Roadhouse

The Great Family Songbook

A Treasury of Favorite Folk Songs, Popular Tunes, Children's
Melodies, International Songs, Hymns, Holiday Jingles, and More

FOR PIANO AND GUITAR

Dan Fox AND Dick Weissman

Illustrated by SARAH WILKINS

BLACK DOG
& LEVENTHAL
PUBLISHERS
NEW YORK

ACKNOWLEDGMENTS

Thanks to Neil Soderstrom, our valiant agent, who kept this project afloat from inception into the able hands of our editor, Judy Pray. Also, thanks to J. P. Leventhal for suggesting this concept and to Laura Ross for cheering us on. We thank Sarah Wilkins for her charming illustrations.

The Great Family Songbook
Text copyright © 2007 by Dan Fox and Dick Weissman
Illustrations copyright © 2007 by Sarah Wilkins

Published by
Black Dog & Leventhal Publishers, Inc.
151 West 19th Street
New York, NY 10011

Distributed by
Workman Publishing Company
225 Varick Street
New York, NY 10014

Design by Susi Oberhelman
Manufactured in China

ISBN-13: 978-1-57912-758-9

g f e d c b a

Library of Congress Cataloging-in-Publication Data is on file at Black Dog & Leventhal Publishers, Inc.

Contents

FOREWORD

By the mid-twentieth century, American popular music had begun to dominate the airwaves of the entire world. In our country's understandable enthusiasm for rock and roll and hip-hop, we have tended to overlook our rich musical heritage.

In this book, we have included a sprinkling of classic American folk rock songs, while concentrating mainly on that wonderful earlier heritage. Here you'll find songs from virtually every American musical genre—from military and patriotic tunes, to folk and country songs, and from Tin Pan Alley and ragtime, to songs from Broadway and Hollywood, along with some widely loved songs that originated outside the United States.

For each song, we've provided complete lyrics with music arranged for both keyboard and chord symbols for guitar. We have also included right-hand strums (accompaniment patterns) in a special section found in the back of the book. The keyboard arrangements are easy for players of even modest skills, and any guitarist with a basic knowledge of chords will have little trouble mastering most of the songs. The professional musician will find the book a valuable resource.

We trust that you, your family, and your friends will enjoy playing and singing these wonderful songs. We've introduced each with a short history, including information on the writer and composer and the year it was created. With the range of songs and the charming illustrations, we hope you'll make the book one of your family treasures. This book reflects our enthusiasm for the many musical styles that we have experienced in our careers as musicians, arrangers, songwriters, and record producers. May it kindle your enthusiasm too.

DAN FOX AND DICK WEISSMAN

American Patriotic Songs

Battle Hymn of the Republic

[*Words by* JULIA WARD HOWE, *music by* WILLIAM STEFFE]

Inspired by Abraham Lincoln's call for volunteers to join the Union Army, Julia Ward Howe wrote the lyrics of this patriotic song in 1861. The Hutchinson Family, a famous antislavery group, was the first to perform it, and it was heard during some of the fiercest battles of the Civil War. The composer was purportedly William Steffe; he based the tune on a camp meeting hymn. The melody is so stirring that two different sets of lyrics were used by the Union forces, one as a rallying cry, the other as a battle song. The Confederate Army created their own version of the lyrics, and so did African-American Union soldiers.

Slow march

1. Mine eyes have seen the glo - ry of the com - ing of the Lord, He is
2. I have seen Him in the watch-fires of a hun-dred circ-ling camps, They have
3. He has sound-ed forth the trum - pet that shall nev - er call re - treat, He is

tramp-ling out the vin - tage where the grapes of wrath are stored; He has
build-ed Him an al - tar in the eve - ning dews and damps; I can
sift - ing out the hearts of men be - fore His judg - ment seat. Oh, be

The Caisson Song

THE CAISSONS GO ROLLING ALONG

[*Words and music by* EDMUND L. GRUBER]

A caisson is a two-wheeled wagon, used for carrying artillery ammunition. Gruber wrote this song when he was a lieutenant serving in the Philippines, soon after the Spanish-American War. Gruber was inspired to write the song after a difficult march his battalion made across a mountain range. He also published an instrumental version in 1918.

March tempo

The Star-Spangled Banner

[*Words by* FRANCIS SCOTT KEY, *music by* JOHN STAFFORD SMITH]

In 1812, the United States fought its second and last war with England. As the war dragged on into 1814, Francis Scott Key, the district attorney for Washington, D.C., was feeling helpless as the British bombarded Fort McHenry in Baltimore. Fearing that the British had captured the American fort, Scott Key was inspired to write this song, which was later sung to an English tune called "To Anacreon in Heaven." In 1931, the song was adopted as the official national anthem of the United States.

Majestically

Oh say can you see by the dawn's ear - ly light What so proud - ly we hailed at the twi - light's last gleam - ing? Whose broad stripes and bright stars through the per - il - ous fight O'er the

Dixie

[*Words and music by* DANIEL DECATUR EMMETT]

There are conflicting versions of the meaning of the word Dixie in this popular Confederate song. One attributes the word to a slave master named Dixie; another claims that a Dixie was a ten-dollar note.

America, the Beautiful

[*Words by* KATHERINE LEE BATES, *music by* SAMUEL A. WARD]

The music for this patriotic song is based on an old hymn entitled "Materna," composed by Samuel Ward, in 1886. Bates was inspired to write the lyrics when she climbed majestic Pikes Peak, in Colorado, in 1893. Although the song was first printed in 1895, Bates rewrote the words in 1904 and again in 1913. This song is held in such high esteem that periodically it is talked of as a replacement for "The Star-Spangled Banner." Hundreds of artists have performed it, and the late Ray Charles turned in a particularly inspired rendition.

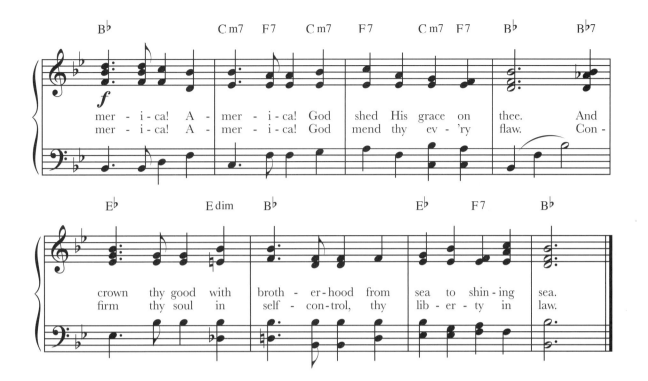

3. O beautiful for heroes proved
   In liberating strife,
   Who more than self their country loved
   And mercy more than life!
   America! America!
   May God thy gold refine,
   'Till all success be nobleness,
   And ev'ry gain divine.

4. O beautiful for patriot dream
   That sees beyond the years
   Thine alabaster cities gleam
   Undimmed by human tears!
   America! America!
   God shed His grace on thee,
   And crown thy good with brotherhood
   From sea to shining sea.

Yankee Doodle

[TRADITIONAL]

The original melody of "Yankee Doodle" is from England and dates to more than a hundred years before the American Revolution. A doodle is defined in old English dictionaries as a fool or simpleton.

Brightly, with spirit

1. Fath'r and I went down to camp a - long with Cap-tain Good-in', And
2. There we saw a thou-sand men, as rich as Squi - er Da - vid; And
3. Yan - kee Doo - dle went to Lon - don rid - ing on a po - ny, He

there we saw the men and boys as thick as has - ty pud - din'.
what they wast - ed ev - 'ry day, I wish it could be sav - èd.
stuck a feath - er in his cap and called it mac - a - ro - ni.

Chorus:

Yan - kee Doo - dle, keep it up! Yan - kee Doo - dle dan - dy.

Mind the mu - sic and the step, and with the girls be han - dy.

When Johnny Comes Marching Home

[*Words by* LOUIS LAMBERT (PATRICK GILMORE), *music* TRADITIONAL IRISH SONG]

Patrick Gilmore was the bandmaster of the Union Army during the Civil War. Using the pen name Louis Lambert, he wrote this stirring song, based on the melody of a traditional Irish antiwar song.

Anchors Aweigh

[*Words by* CHARLES A. ZIMMERMAN, *music by* ALFRED HART MILES]

The first performance of this song took place at the Army-Navy football game in 1906. Zimmerman was a lieutenant and a former bandmaster at the Naval Academy, where Miles was a midshipman. Miles asked Zimmerman to help him to polish the song. The original intent of the writers was to create a march for football games, and although the song has no official status, it is probably the best-known naval song and is often used at high school athletic competitions too.

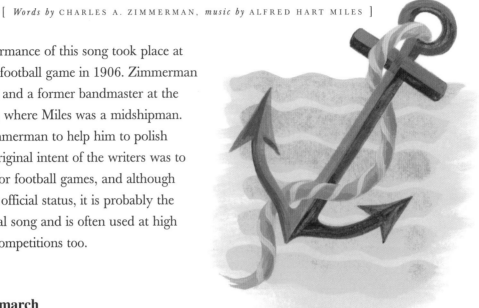

Spirited march

You're a Grand Old Flag

[*Words and music by* GEORGE M. COHAN]

This song was inspired a Civil War veteran, who used the phrase "it's a grand old rag." Cohan changed the word "rag" to "flag" when patriotic Americans expressed outrage at the term.

Brightly, with spirit

You're a grand old flag, you're a high-fly - ing flag, And for - ev - er in peace may you wave. You're the em - blem of the land I love, The

Over There

[Words and music by GEORGE M. COHAN *]*

When the United States entered World War I in April 1917, Broadway songsmith George M. Cohan was immediately inspired to write this patriotic anthem. The song became so revered that Cohan was awarded a Congressional Medal of Honor for writing it.

Brightly, like a march

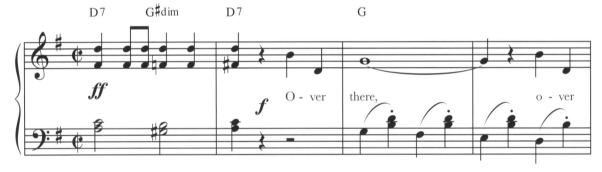

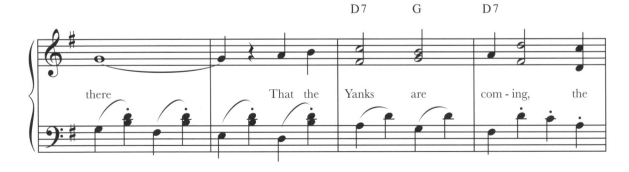

Marines' Hymn

[AUTHOR UNKNOWN]

The melody of this song is taken from Offenbach's comic opera *Genevieve de Brabant*. Although no one knows who wrote the lyrics, supposedly a marine on duty in Mexico wrote it just after the end of the war between the United States and Mexico in 1848. The phrase "the halls of Montezuma" refers to the United States defeat of the Mexicans in the home of the Aztec king, and "the shores of Tripoli" is a reference to the 1805 war against the Barbary pirates operating off the North African coast. The "Marines' Hymn" has been sung and played wherever the U.S. Marines have landed.

This Land Is Your Land

[*Word and music by* WOODY GUTHRIE]

Woody Guthrie originally wrote this song as a response to Irving Berlin's tune "God Bless America." It was Woody's intention to come up with something more down to earth that could appeal to the average American. He first wrote the song in 1940, and he recorded it in 1944. The melody can be traced back to an old hymn titled "When the World's on Fire" and also to a Carter Family song titled "Little Darlin' Pal of Mine." The original version contained two verses protesting economic equality that are rarely sung today.

Moderately bright

America

MY COUNTRY 'TIS OF THEE

[*Words by* SAMUEL F. SMITH, *music* TRADITIONAL]

In 1832, Smith was inspired by a German hymnal melody to write this timeless patriotic song.

Slow and stately

Western, Cowboy, & Hoedown Songs

Red River Valley

[TRADITIONAL]

The song is popular in both the United States and Canada, and it is variously regarded as a song about the sorrow of a local Canadian woman as her beloved soldier is leaving and a folk version of a Texas song called "In the Bright Mohawk Valley."

Loping along

Buffalo Gals

[*Words and music by* COOL WHITE (JOHN HODGES)]

Buffalo Gals" is a nineteenth-century minstrel song. It was written by a performer named John Hodges and published in 1844. During this era, white performers painted their faces black and imitated African-American dances, dialect, and songs. When the minstrel show moved to another town, the title was changed to the name of the new city. According to folklorist Frank Brown, the tune may have come from a German music hall song and the lyrics from an English children's game.

Brightly, with spirit

1. As   I   was   walk - ing   down   the   street,
2. I   asked   her   would   she   have   some   talk,
3. I   asked   her   would   she   like   to   dance,

The Farmer Is the Man

[TRADITIONAL]

Fiddlin' John Carson, one of the pioneer country and western artists, recorded this complaint about the lot of the poor farmer in the early 1920s. The song dates from the 1870s, when the Midwest Farmer's Alliance tried to organize farmers to protest against the low prices paid for their crops. The song describes the difficulties of making a living as a farmer, and it has retained its popularity for many years.

1. When the far-mer comes to town with his wag-on bro-ken down, Oh, the
2. When the law-yer hangs a-round while the butch-er cuts a pound, Oh, the

far - mer is the man who feeds them all. If you'll
far - mer is the man who feeds them all. And the

only look and see, I think you will a-gree That the
preach-er and the cook go a-stroll-ing by the brook, Oh, the

G7   C7   F

far - mer is the man who feeds them all. The
far - mer is the man who feeds them all. The

far - mer is the man, the far - mer is the man, lives on cred-it till the
far - mer is the man, the far - mer is the man, lives on cred-it till the

fall. Then they take him by the hand and they lead him from the land, And the
fall. With the int-'rest rate so high, it's a won-der he don't die, for the

G7   C7   F

mid - dle-man's the man who gets it all.
mort - gage man's the man who gets it all.

Git Along Little Dogies

[TRADITIONAL]

In 1893, novelist Owen Wister, author of *The Virginian,* wrote some verses to this song in his diary. He had heard the song in Texas, and he faithfully transcribed it. Later the song appeared in John Lomax's cowboy song collection *Cowboy Songs and Other Frontier Ballads.* Folklorist John White even titled an entire collection of cowboy songs, *Git Along Little Dogies, Songs and Songmakers of the American West,* after this song.

1. As I was a-walk-ing one morn-ing for plea-sure, I spied a cow-punch-er a-rid-ing a-long. His hat was thrown back and his spurs were a-jing-lin', And
2. It's ear-ly in spring that we round up the do-gies, We mark them and brand them and bob off their tails. We round up our hors-es, load up the chuck wag-on, And
3. It's whoop-ing and yell-ing and driv-in' the do-gies, And oh how I wish you would on-ly go on. It's whoop-ing and punch-ing, go on, lit-tle do-gies, You

The Old Chisholm Trail

[TRADITIONAL]

Old Chisholm Trail" is one of the most popular cowboy songs of all time. Hundreds of verses have been collected by folklorists. The trail is named after Jesse Chisholm and dates from 1867. It ran from Abilene, Kansas, to San Antonio, Texas. Thousands of head of cattle were herded across several rivers running between Texas and Kansas, on long and fabled cattle drives that have been chronicled in movies and literature.

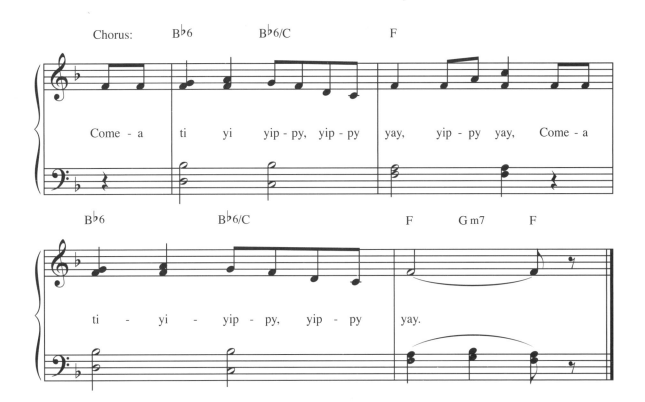

Chorus: B♭6   B♭6/C   F

Come - a ti yi yip - py, yip - py yay, yip - py yay, Come - a

B♭6   B♭6/C   F   G m7   F

ti - yi - yip - py, yip - py yay.

4. Oh, it's bacon and beans
   Most ev'ry day;
   We'll soon be eating
   This prairie hay:
   (repeat chorus)

5. I went to the boss
   To draw my roll;
   He had me figured out
   Ten dollars in the hole:
   (repeat chorus)

6. With my seat in the saddle
   And my hand on the horn
   I'm the best cowpuncher
   That ever was born:
   (repeat chorus)

7. With my knees in the saddle
   And my seat in the sky
   I'll quit punchin' cows
   In the sweet by and by:
   (repeat chorus)

Home on the Range

[*Words by* BREWSTER HIGLEY, *music by* DAN KELLY]

This American classic had its origins in a poem called "My Kansas Home," written by Kansan Brewster Higley in 1871. A neighbor found the poem and enlisted a local fiddler named Dan Kelly to write a tune for it. The song spread far and wide, and in different states the title was changed to reflect the singer's home state. In 1947, it was adopted as the state song of Kansas.

Moderately

1. Oh, give me a home where the buf - fa - lo roam, Where the
2. How of - ten at night when the heav - ens are bright With the
3. Oh, give me a land where the bright dia - mond sand Flows

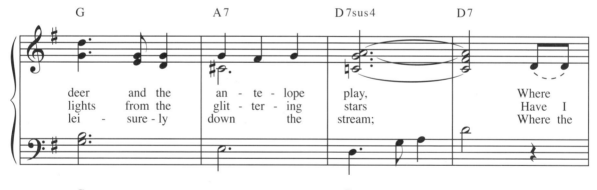

deer and the an - te - lope play, Where
lights from the glit - ter - ing stars Have I
lei - sure - ly down the stream; Where the

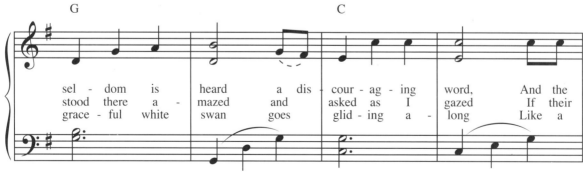

sel - dom is heard a dis - cour - ag - ing word, And the
stood there a - mazed and asked as I gazed If their
grace - ful white swan goes glid - ing a - long Like a

Oh! Susanna

[*Words and music by* STEPHEN FOSTER]

Stephen Foster is regarded as America's first professional songwriter. Although such classics as "Camptown Races" and "My Old Kentucky Home" sold thousands of copies of sheet music, Foster remained poverty stricken and nearly indigent, dying at the age of thirty-eight. This song, written in 1848, became extremely popular during the California Gold Rush of 1849, with the lyrics changed from "Oh! Susanna" to "Oh! California."

Brightly

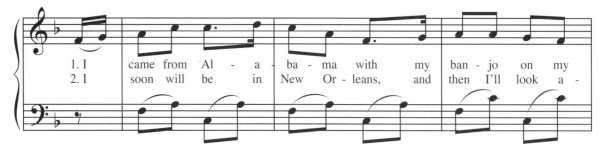

Verses:

1. I came from Al- a- ba- ma with my ban- jo on my
2. I soon will be in New Or- leans, and then I'll look a-

Sweet Betsy from Pike

[TRADITIONAL]

There are dozens of versions of this California Gold Rush tune, which adopted the melody of an old English ballad called "Villikins and His Dinah." Pike refers to Pike County, Missouri, and the song traces the odyssey of Betsy and her lover Ike, as they make their tortuous way to California, marry, and then divorce. The song pokes fun at both Betsy and Ike and their long adventure. "Sweet Betsy from Pike" is an accurate historical depiction of the westward expansion experience. There are many different sets of lyrics written for this song.

With spirit

mf

Verses:

1. Oh, will you re - mem - ber sweet Bet - sy from Pike? She
2. One eve - ning quite ear - ly they camped on the Platte. 'Twas
3. The Shang - hai ran off and their cat - tle all died; That

crossed the high moun - tains with her lov - er Ike. With
near by the road on a green shad - y flat. Where
morn - ing the last piece of ba - con was fried. Poor

two yoke of ox - en And a big yal - ler dog, A
Bet - sy, sore - foot - ed lay down to re - pose; With
Ike was dis - cour - aged and Bet - sy got mad; The

tall Shang - hai roos - ter and one spot - ted hog.
won - der Ike gazed on his Pike Coun - ty rose.
dog drooped his tail and looked won - d'rous - ly sad.

Chorus:

Hoo - dle dang fol - de di - do, hoo-dle dang fol - de - day.

4. They soon reached the desert where Betsy gave out,
   And down in the sand she lay rolling about,
   While Ike, half-distracted, looked on in surprise,
   Saying, "Betsy, get up, you'll get sand in your eyes."
   (repeat chorus)

5. Sweet Betsy got up in a great deal of pain,
   Declared she'd go back to Pike County again.
   But Ike gave a sigh, and they fondly embraced,
   And they traveled along with his arm round her waist.
   (repeat chorus)

6. Now won't you remember sweet Betsy from Pike?
   She crossed the high mountains with her lover, Ike.
   With two yoke of oxen, a big yaller dog,
   A tall Shanghai rooster and one spotted hog.
   (repeat chorus)

She'll Be Comin' 'round the Mountain

[TRADITIONAL]

This old favorite was based on an African-American spiritual called "When the Chariot Comes." After the song spread through Appalachia, the lyrics were transformed into the version we sing today. Because the ends of the lines are repeated with great energy, children usually enjoy shouting out the words to this tune.

Brightly, with spirit

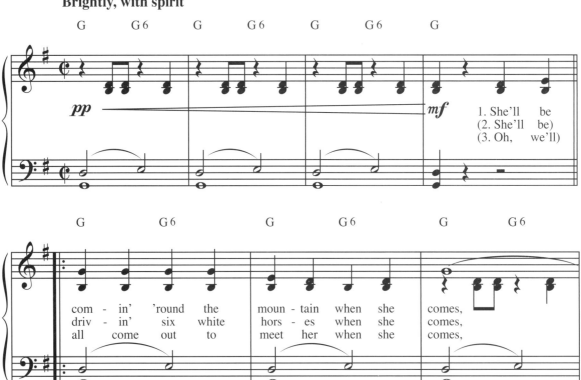

1. She'll be
(2. She'll be)
(3. Oh, we'll)

com - in' 'round the moun - tain when she comes,
driv - in' six white hors - es when she comes,
all come out to meet her when she comes,

Clementine

[AUTHOR UNKNOWN]

Clementine" has been credited variously to Percy Montrose and Baker Bradford. It dates from 1884, although some believe it to be borrowed from an earlier song called "Down by the River Liv'd a Maiden," written by H. S. Thompson in 1863. The lyrics poke gentle fun at a California "miner '49'er" and his daughter Clementine.

Moderately fast

Verses:

1. In a cav - ern, in a can - yon, Ex - ca -
2. Light she was and like a fai - ry And her
3. Drove she duck - lings to the wa - ter Ev - 'ry

vat - ing for a mine, Lived a min - er, for - ty -
shoes were num - ber nine; Her - ring box - es with - out
morn - ing just at nine; Hit her foot a - gainst a

4. Ruby lips above the water
   Blowing bubbles soft and fine;
   But alas, I was no swimmer,
   So I lost my Clementine.
   (repeat chorus)

5. In a churchyard near the canyon
   Where the myrtle doth entwine
   There grew roses and the posies
   Fertilized by Clementine.
   (repeat chorus)

Turkey in the Straw

[TRADITIONAL]

Although we refer to this as a traditional song, there are numerous unsubstantiated claims of authorship by several minstrel-era performers of the early nineteenth century. This tune is sometimes performed as an instrumental and sometimes sung with lyrics. The earliest lyrics for the song were written by Dan Bryant of Bryant's Minstrels, and it was published in 1834.

Hoedown tempo

Verses:
1. As
2. I
3. As

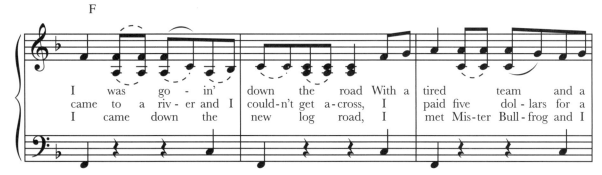

I was go - in' down the road With a tired team and a
came to a riv - er and I could - n't get a - cross, I
I came down the new log road, I

paid five dol - lars for a
met Mis - ter Bull - frog and I

heav - y load, I crack my whip and the lead - er sprung, I
blind ol' hoss; He would-n't go a-head and he would-n't stand still, So he
met Miss Toad. And ev - 'ry time Miss Toad would sing, Ol'

says day - day to the wag - on tongue.
went up and down like an old saw mill!
Bull - frog cut a pi - geon wing!

Chorus:

Tur-key in the straw, tur-key in the hay; Tur-key in the straw,

tur-key in the hay! Roll 'em up, twist 'em up, high tuck-a-haw, And

play 'em up a tune called "Tur - key in the Straw."

Jesse James

[TRADITIONAL]

Missouri natives Jesse James and his brother Frank, along with the Younger Brothers, formed the James Gang after the end of the Civil War. They developed something of a legendary reputation for stealing from the rich and rewarding the poor. Throughout a fifteen-year period they robbed numerous banks and railroads all the way from Minnesota to Texas. Jesse met his demise at the hands of "that dirty little coward" Robert Ford in 1882. Ford didn't live happily ever after either; he was killed in a gunfight in the mining town of Creed, Colorado, in 1892.

Brightly, with spirit

Verses:

1. Jes - se James was a lad who killed man-y a
2. It was with his broth - er Frank they robbed the Gal - la - tin
3. It was on a Wedn's-day night, the moon was shin - ing

man; He robbed the Glen - dale train.
bank, And car - ried the mon - ey from the town.
bright, They robbed the Glen - dale train.

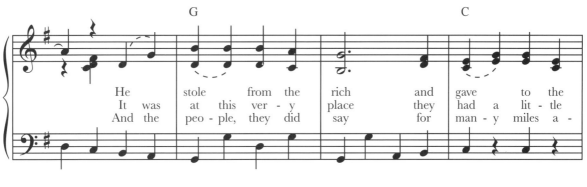

He stole from the rich and gave to the
It was at this ver - y place and they
And the peo - ple, they did say for man - y miles a -

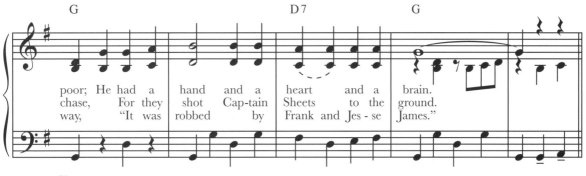

poor; He had a hand and a heart and a brain.
chase, For they shot Cap-tain Sheets to the ground.
way, "It was robbed by Frank and Jes - se James."

Chorus:

Poor Jes - se had a wife to mourn for his life, two

4. They went to the crossing, not very far from here,
   And there they did the same;
   With the agent on his knees, he delivered up the keys
   To the outlaws, Frank and Jesse James.
   (repeat chorus)

5. Well, the people held their breath
   When they heard of Jesse's death
   And wondered how he came to die.
   It was one of the gang called little Robert Ford;
   He shot poor Jesse on the sly.
   (repeat chorus)

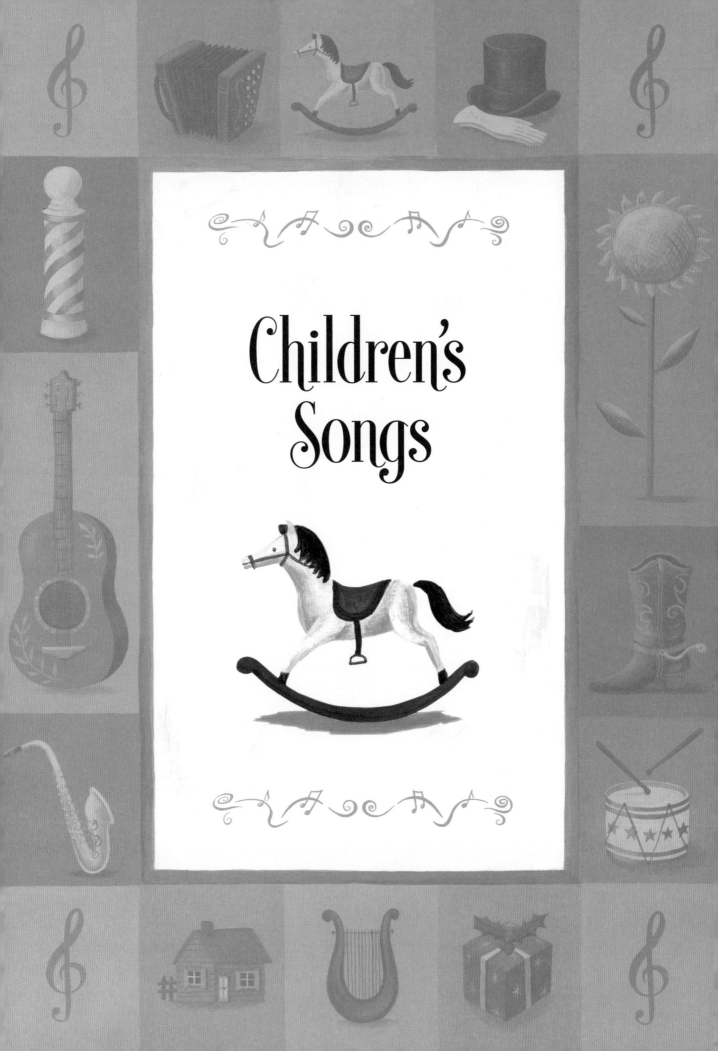

Children's Songs

Hush Little Baby

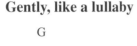

[TRADITIONAL]

One of the most famous of all children's songs in the English language, this song has been reprinted in countless songbooks. Although the original source for the song is unknown, it is believed to have originated as a Southern party song that was used in children's games.

Gently, like a lullaby

5. If that billy goat don't pull,
   Poppa's gonna buy you a cart and bull.

6. And if that cart and bull turn over,
   Poppa's gonna buy you a dog named Rover.

7. And if that dog named Rover won't bark,
   Poppa's gonna buy you a horse and cart.

8. And if that horse and cart fall down,
   You'll still be the sweetest little baby in town.

Twinkle, Twinkle, Little Star

[T R A D I T I O N A L]

This favorite was originally an eighteenth-century French song called "Ah Vous Dirai-Je, Maman (Mother I Would Tell You)." Mozart used the melody in one of his piano variations and Jane Taylor wrote the English version in 1806.

Not too slow

1. Twin - kle, twin - kle, lit - tle star; How I won - der what you are.
2. When the blaz - ing sun is gone, When he noth - ing shines up - on,

Up a - bove the world so high, Like a dia - mond in the sky,
Then you show your lit - tle light, Twin - kle, twin - kle all the night.

Twin - kle, twin - kle, lit - tle star, How I won - der what you are.
Twin - kle, twin - kle, lit - tle star, How I won - der what you are.

3. Then the trav'ler in the dark
   Thanks you for your tiny spark;
   He could not see where to go
   If you did not twinkle so.
   Twinkle, twinkle, little star,
   How I wonder what you are.

4. In the dark blue sky you keep
   While you thro' my window peep.
   And you never shut your eye
   Till the sun is in the sky.
   Twinkle, twinkle, little star,
   How I wonder what you are.

The Wheels on the Bus

[TRADITIONAL]

The person leading this song asks kids to imitate the sounds that a bus or its passengers make. The song includes mention of the windshield wipers, the brakes, and whatever else the leader may indicate.

Not too fast

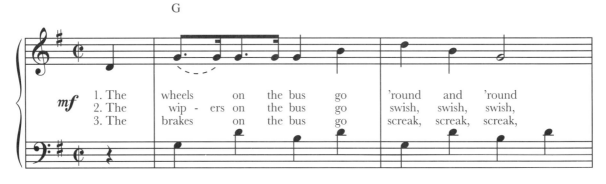

1. The wheels on the bus go 'round and 'round
2. The wip - ers on the bus go swish, swish, swish,
3. The brakes on the bus go screak, screak, screak,

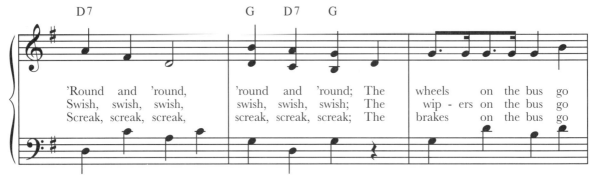

'Round and 'round, 'round and 'round; The wheels on the bus go
Swish, swish, swish, swish, swish, swish; The wip - ers on the bus go
Screak, screak, screak, screak, screak, screak; The brakes on the bus go

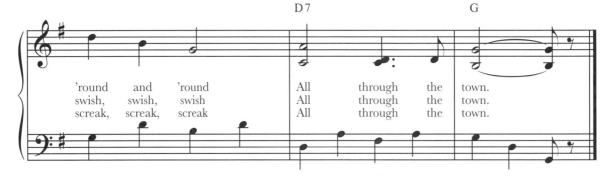

'round and 'round   All through the town.
swish, swish, swish   All through the town.
screak, screak, screak   All through the town.

4. The babies on the bus go wah, wah, wah,
   Wah, wah, wah, wah, wah, wah;
   The babies on the bus go wah, wah, wah
   All through the town.

CONTINUE SIMILARLY:

5. The mommies on the bus go shh, shh, shh . . .
6. The children on the bus go up and down . . .
7. The driver on the bus goes, "Move on back". . .

This Old Man

[TRADITIONAL]

Originally known as a nursery rhyme, "This Old Man" gained a new lease on life through its use in the 1958 film *The Inn of the Sixth Happiness,* starring Ingrid Bergman.

CONTINUE SIMILARLY:

four . . . door
five . . . hive
six . . . sticks
seven . . . up in heav'n
eight . . . plate
nine . . . spine
ten . . . over again

Old MacDonald

[TRADITIONAL]

This is an audience-participation song, where children delight in singing animal noises in the chorus. The earliest version of this old chestnut has been traced to Thomas D'Urfey's *Wit and Mirth: Pills to Purge Melancholy*, which was published in England in 1719. American versions that are closer to the song are found in Vance Randolph's books of Ozark mountain songs and Frank Brown's collections of songs from North Carolina.

Brightly, with spirit

1. Old Mac-Don-ald had a farm, E - I - E - I - O. And
2. Old Mac-Don-ald had a farm, E - I - E - I - O. And

on this farm he had some chicks, E - I - E - I - O. With a
on this farm he had some ducks, E - I - E - I - O. With a

chick - chick here, and a chick - chick there;
quack - quack here, and a quack - quack there;

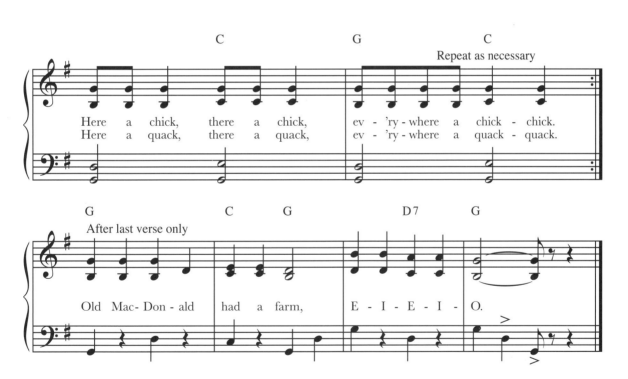

CONTINUE SIMILARLY:

3. cows . . . moo moo

4. pigs . . . oink oink

5. sheep . . . baa baa

6. cats . . . meow meow

7. dogs . . . ruff ruff

8. donkeys . . . hee haw

9. horses . . . neigh neigh

10. mice . . . squeak squeak

11. giraffes . . . (stay silent)

12. geese . . . honk honk

Eency Weency Spider

[TRADITIONAL]

While singing this song, children can imitate the spider's actions described in the lyrics.

Not too fast

The een-cy, ween-sy spi-der went up the wa-ter-spout;

Down came the rain and washed the spi-der out;

Out came the sun and dried up all the rain, And the

een-cy, ween-sy spi-der went up the spout a-gain.

B-I-N-G-O

[TRADITIONAL]

B- I- N- G- O" is an activity song that can help children learn how to spell.

Brightly, with spirit

For the third verse clap for B, I, and N.
For the fourth verse clap for B, I, N, and G.
For the fifth and last verse clap for all the letters in Bingo's name.

All the Pretty Little Horses

[TRADITIONAL]

There is a marked disparity between the soothing melody of this beautiful lullaby and the striking lyrics of the second verse of the song. This verse concerns a poor lamb that is being frightened by "bees and butterflies." This change in the point of view in the verses reflects the fact that the singer is a Southern African-American woman who is taking care of her master's children, while her own "poor lambs" are neglected.

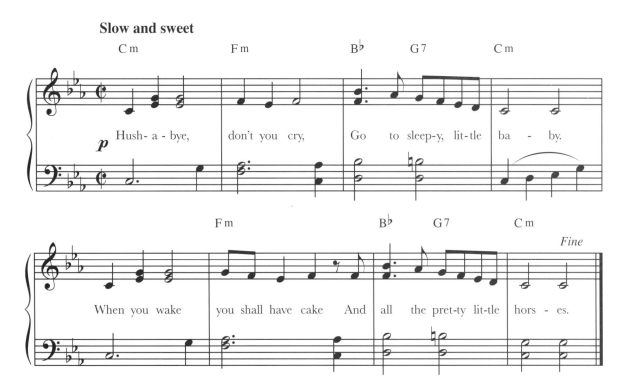

Slow and sweet

Cm Fm Bb G7 Cm

p Hush-a-bye, don't you cry, Go to sleep-y, lit-tle ba - by.

Fm Bb G7 Cm

Fine

When you wake you shall have cake And all the pret-ty lit-tle hors - es.

If You're Happy and You Know It

[TRADITIONAL]

While the song leader sings the words to this traditional song or nursery rhyme, children follow the leader's directions to clap their hands, stomp their feet, or do whatever else the leader suggests. This song has been altered through the years and the lyrics changed to show religious and political emphasis.

Moderately

1. If you're hap-py and you know it clap your hands (clap clap); If you're hap-py and you know it clap your hands (clap clap); If you're hap-py and you know it and you real-ly wan-na show it, If you're

2. If you're hap-py and you know it stomp your feet (stomp stomp); If you're hap-py and you know it stomp your feet (stomp stomp); If you're hap-py and you know it and you real-ly wan-na show it, If you're

3. If you're hap-py and you know it shout hoo-ray (hoo-ray!); If you're hap-py and you know it shout hoo-ray (hoo-ray!); If you're hap-py and you know it and you real-ly wan-na show it, If you're

The Noble Duke of York

[TRADITIONAL]

This song is about a real person, although there is some controversy as to *which* Duke of York is depicted here. Most musicologists believe that the duke was Frederick Augustus, the second son of George III, who was the king of England at the time of the American Revolution. Frederick Augustus was a military commander, who lived from 1763 to 1827. There doesn't appear to be any evidence that the clown-like behavior attributed to him in the song is accurate.

March tempo

Skip to My Lou

[TRADITIONAL]

To dance to "Skip To My Lou," traditionally couples form a circle around a single boy, in tribute to his losing his dance partner. During the dance the isolated boy borrows the female partner of one of the dancers and the displaced male dancer finds his way into the circle. In the last verse a "greenie" refers to a boy or girl without a dance partner.

Bright hoedown tempo

Verses:

Fly in the but-ter-milk, shoo, fly, shoo!
Lost my part-ner, what-'ll I do?
I'll get an-oth-er one pret-ti-er than you,

Fly in the but-ter-milk, shoo, fly, shoo!
Lost my part-ner, what-'ll I do?
I'll get an-oth-er one pret-ti-er than you,

Fly in the but-ter-milk,
Lost my part-ner,
I'll get an-oth-er one

shoo, fly, shoo! | Skip to my Lou, my dar - lin'.
what - 'll I do? | Skip to my Lou, my dar - lin'.
pret - ti - er than you, | Skip to my Lou, my dar - lin'.

Chorus:

Skip, skip, skip to my Lou, | Skip, skip, skip to my Lou,

Skip, skip, skip to my Lou, | Skip to my Lou, my dar - lin'.

4. Little red wagon painted blue,
   Little red wagon painted blue,
   Little red wagon painted blue,
   Skip to my Lou, my darlin'.
   (repeat chorus)

5. Look at the greenie standing there,
   Look at the greenie standing there,
   Look at the greenie standing there,
   Skip to my Lou, my darlin'.

Brahms's Lullaby

[*Words* TRADITIONAL, *music by* JOHANNES BRAHMS]

Brahms wrote this beautiful melody in 1868, based on the tune of an old Austrian song. The song was composed in honor of the first child of one of Brahms's close Viennese friends.

Gently

Lul-la - by and good night, with ros - es be - dight, With lil - ies be - decked is ba - by's wee bed. Lay thee down now and rest, May thy slum - ber be blessed. Lay thee down now and rest, may thy slum - ber be blessed.

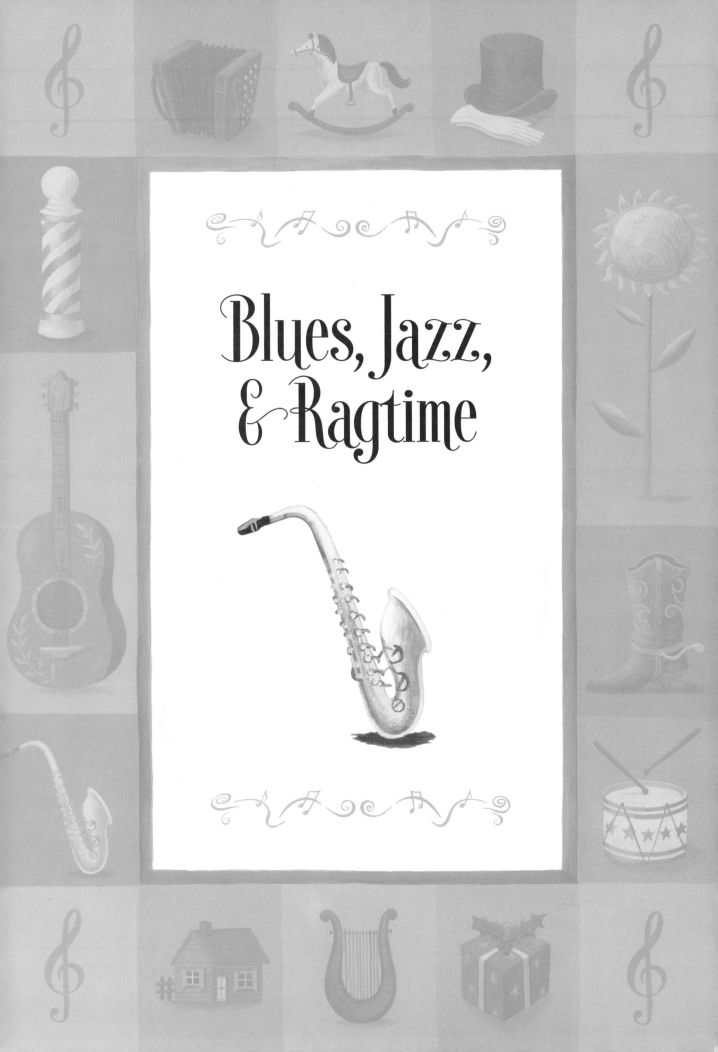

Blues, Jazz, & Ragtime

Careless Love

[TRADITIONAL]

The song "Careless Love" has appeared in a number of musical guises. It has been recorded as a plaintive country ballad by artists such as Joan Baez, Elvis Presley, and Johnny Cash. And it has had another life as a blues or rhythm and blues song recorded by artists such as Josh White, Bessie Smith, Fats Domino, Dave Van Ronk, Leadbelly, Janis Joplin, and Bob Dylan. W. C. Handy wrote his own version, using the title "Loveless Love."

4. Now I wear my apron high,
   Now I wear my apron high,
   Now I wear my apron high,
   You see my door and pass it by.

5. Cried last night and the night before,
   Cried last night and the night before,
   Cried last night, the night before,
   I'll cry tonight and cry no more.

Alexander's Ragtime Band

[*Words and music by* IRVING BERLIN]

Irving Berlin was probably the most successful songwriter of the twentieth century. This song was his first real hit, written in 1911. Although the lyrics of the song refer to African-American musicians, as does the title, the tune is not, in fact, a rag. A 1938 movie uses the song as the title of the film, and Berlin himself was one of the authors of the screenplay.

nev- er heard be-fore, So nat - u - ral that you want to go to war;

C   F#dim   G 7   C

That's just   the   best - est   band   what   am,

C7   F

hon - ey lamb!   Come on   a - long,   come on a-

House of the Rising Sun

[TRADITIONAL]

Some people say that this house is one of prostitution, but blues singer Dave Van Ronk claimed to have seen pictures of a New Orleans women's prison that had an entrance decorated with a rising sun.

Bill Bailey

[*Words and music by* HUGHIE CANNON]

Cannon was a songwriter and pianist, and this song became a jazz standard. The lyrics portray a no-good male chauvinist whose charms are irresistible, even to the woman he has mistreated. Country singer Patsy Cline, jazz singer Ella Fitzgerald, Brenda Lee, Bobby Darin, and Louis Armstrong are just a few of the many artists who recorded this song.

Brightly, with spirit

"Won't you come home, Bill Bai-ley, won't you come home?"

mf

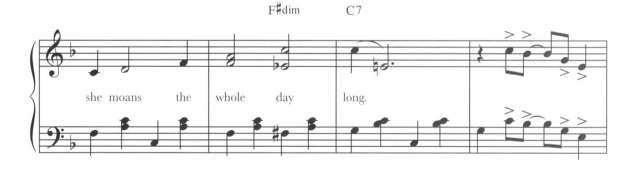

she moans the whole day long.

"I'll do the cook-in', dar-lin', I'll pay the rent;

Frankie and Johnny

[TRADITIONAL]

Scholars claim that this tragic song is based on an actual event—the travails of a couple named Albert Britt and Frances (Frankie) Baker. She shot him to death in 1899, and some versions of the song, notably one by the great songster Mississippi John Hurt, use the title "Frankie and Albert." Dozens of verses have been collected, and Elvis Presley starred in a movie about the ill-fated couple, which was released in 1966.

Moderately, with a swing

1. Frank - ie and John - ny were sweet - hearts,
2. Frank - ie went down to the cor - ner,
3. "Don't want to cause you no trou - ble;

Oh, Lord - y, how they could love;   They
Just for a buck - et of beer;   She
Don't want to tell you no lie.   But

4. Frankie looked over the transom
   And found to her great surprise
   That there on the bed sat Johnny,
   Makin' love to Nellie Bly.
   He was her man,
   But he done her wrong.

5. Frankie drew back her kimono,
   She took out her big forty-four,
   Rooty-toot-toot, that gal did shoot
   Right through that hardwood door;
   He was her man,
   But he done her wrong.

6. "Roll me over real easy,
   Roll me over real slow.
   Roll me on my right side,
   'Cause the bullet hurts me so.
   I was your man,
   But I was doin' you wrong."

7. Frankie went up to his coffin,
   She looked down upon his face.
   Said, "Lord, have mercy on me;
   I wish that I could take his place.
   He was my man,
   But I done him wrong!"

St. Louis Blues

[*Words and music by* W. C. HANDY]

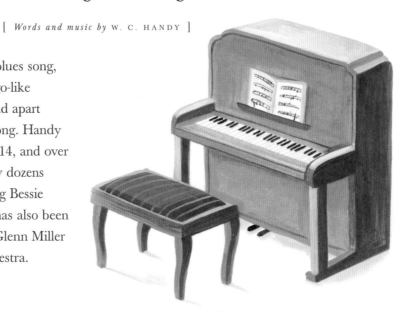

Although this is basically a blues song, Handy ingeniously added a tango-like section. This made the song stand apart from virtually any other blues song. Handy published the song himself in 1914, and over the years it has been recorded by dozens of blues and jazz greats, including Bessie Smith and Louis Armstrong. It has also been recorded instrumentally by the Glenn Miller Band and the Boston Pops Orchestra.

Moderately

Pretty Baby

[*Words by* GUS KAHN, *music by* EGBERT VAN ALSTYNE *and* TONY JACKSON]

It is not entirely clear who wrote this song. Legend says that Jackson, a noted ragtime pianist, wrote the chorus, and the contribution of Van Alstyne, who achieved some success as a Tin Pan Alley songwriter, is not entirely clear. Four different movies have used the title of the song, including the 1978 film by French film auteur Louis Malle.

Moderately, with a lilt

Ev - 'ry - bod - y loves a ba - by, that's why I'm in love with you, Pret - ty

ba - by, pret - ty ba - by. And I'd

like to be your sis - ter, broth - er, dad and moth - er too, Pret - ty

Swanee

[*Words by* IRVING CAESAR, *music by* GEORGE GERSHWIN]

Although George Gershwin is best known today for his opera *Porgy and Bess* and his concerto *Rhapsody in Blue*, he was fully capable of writing hit songs. His first big hit was "Swanee," which was written in 1919 with lyricist Irving Caesar and is twelve minutes long. At the time of writing it, Gershwin was twenty years old, and the song debuted in a musical review called *Demi-Tasse*. Al Jolson heard Gershwin sing it at a party, and then he recorded it too. Because of Jolson's recording, the song sold a million copies of sheet music and more than a million records. Judy Garland was among many artists who later recorded "Swanee."

Put Your Arms around Me, Honey

[*Words by* JUNIE MCCREE, *music by* ALBERT VON TILZER]

Blossom Seely introduced this song to the vaudeville circuit in 1910. Later that year it was interpolated in the musical *Madame Sherry*. This song made its way into various movies, including *Old Oklahoma*, a 1943 film starring John Wayne, and a performance by Judy Garland in the 1949 film *In the Good Old Summertime*. Von Tilzer and his brother Harry each wrote and published many hundreds of songs, and one of Albert's other major hits was "Take Me Out to the Ball Game."

Moderately, with a lilt

Put your arms a - round me, hon - ey, hold me tight;

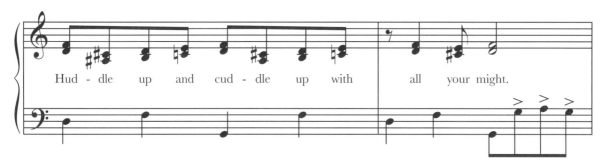

Hud - dle up and cud - dle up with all your might.

Oh, babe, won't you roll those eyes.

Lonesome Road

[TRADITIONAL]

This rendition of this song is based on an African-American spiritual and was recorded by Louis Armstrong, among others. A bluesier version with a different melody has also been recorded.

Nice and bluesy, but not too slow

4. Look up, look up and greet your Maker
'Fore Gabriel blows his horn.

5. Look down, look down, it's weary walkin'
Down that lonesome road.

6. Look up, look up and greet your Maker
'Fore Gabriel blows his horn.

Film & Show Tunes

Meet Me in St. Louis

[*Words by* ANDREW B. STERLING, *music by* KERRY MILLS]

This song was introduced at the St. Louis World's Fair in 1904. The fair celebrated the purchase of the Louisiana Territory. The word is pronounced Loo-ee, which is the French pronunciation.

Bright waltz tempo

Meet me in Saint Lou - is, Lou - is,

Meet me at the fair.

Don't tell me the lights are shin - ing

Give My Regards to Broadway

[*Words and music by* GEORGE M. COHAN]

George M. Cohan wrote this song in 1904 for his musical play *Little Johnny Jones*. There is a definite ragtime flavor to the melody, and because Cohan spent his life as a producer, performer, and songwriter, in a sense the lyrics typify his own life. An early recording was done by Billy Murray, and the song is featured in the 1942 film about Cohan's life *Yankee Doodle Dandy*.

Brightly, with spirit

The Aba Daba Honeymoon

[*Words and music by* ARTHUR FIELDS *and* WALTER DONALDSON]

Written and published in 1914, this song appeared in the 1950 movie *Two Weeks with Love*. It ascended to the number 3 spot on the Billboard chart in 1951. A real pre–rock-and-roll relic, the lyrics of the song mean less than nothing, but the upbeat performance by Debbie Reynolds carried it up the Hit Parade.

Moderately, with spirit

"Ab-a, dab-a, dab-a, dab-a, dab-a, dab-a dab," Said the chimp-ie to the monk. "Bab-a, dab-a, dab-a, dab-a, dab-a, dab-a dab," Said the mon-key to the chimp. All night long they'd chat-ter a-way, All day long they were hap-py and gay,

Ain't We Got Fun

[*Words and music by* RICHARD A. WHITING, RAYMOND EGAN, *and* GUS KAHN]

Published in 1921, this song has not only been recorded by numerous artists, but the lyrics are quoted in F. Scott Fitzgerald's novel *The Great Gatsby*. The composer Richard Whiting was the father of Margaret Whiting, who was an outstanding pop singer of the 1950s.

Moderately

Ev - 'ry morn - ing, ev - 'ry eve - ning, Ain't we got

fun; Not much mon - ey, Oh, but hon - ey,

Ain't we got fun. The rent's un -

paid, dear, we have-n't a bus;

But smiles were made, dear, for peo-ple like

us. In the win-ter, in the sum-mer,

Look for the Silver Lining

[*Words by* BUDDY DE SYLVA, *music by* JEROME KERN]

Composer of hundreds of songs, Jerome Kern was one of the greatest American composers of twentieth-century popular music. Although this song was originally written for another show, Kern recycled it for the 1920 hit Broadway show *Sally,* and it became a film in 1929. Kern also collaborated with Oscar Hammerstein II, writing the 1927 play *Show Boat,* and he continued his winning ways in Broadway shows and Hollywood films alike. Among the many recordings of the song are offerings by jazzman Chet Baker, blues singer Alberta Hunter, pop singers Marion Harris and Judy Garland, and radio raconteur Garrison Keillor.

Moderately, smoothly

Alice Blue Gown

[*Words and music by* JOSEPH MCCARTHY *and* HARRY TIERNEY]

Dedicated to Alice Roosevelt Longworth, the daughter of President Theodore Roosevelt, this song was written for the Broadway musical *Irene,* which debuted in 1919. The show later became a motion picture starring Anna Neagle and Ray Milland. Alice blue is a light blue-gray or steel blue color, which is supposedly one that Ms. Roosevelt Longworth favored.

Moderate waltz tempo

In my sweet lit-tle Al-ice blue gown, When I

first wan-dered down in-to town, I was

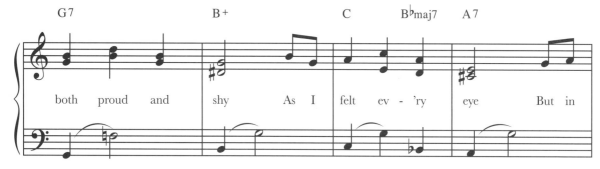

both proud and shy As I felt ev-'ry eye But in

I'm Just Wild about Harry

[*Words by* NOBLE SISSLE, *music by* EUBIE BLAKE]

Sissle and Blake were two African-American songwriters who wrote several hit Broadway musicals, including *Shuffle Along*. "I'm Just Wild about Harry" was featured in the show, which was the first Broadway musical ever to be written and directed by African Americans.

Brightly

mf Oh, I'm just wild a-bout Har - ry, And Har - ry's wild a - bout me. The heav'n - ly bliss - - es of his kiss - - es fill me with ec - - sta - cy. He's

For Me and My Gal

[*Words by* EDGAR LESLIE *and* E. RAY GOETZ, *music by* GEORGE W. MEYER]

Originally written in 1917, the song was revived in the Hollywood musical of the same name. The movie, which starred Judy Garland and was directed by Busby Berkeley, was a major success. The plot featured a vaudeville troupe, with Garland singing and Gene Kelly dancing. The movie included some other major songs of the period, such as "Till We Meet Again" and "It's a Long Way to Tipperary."

Moderately

The bells are ring - ing for me and my gal, The birds are

sing - ing for me and my gal. Ev - 'ry-bod-y's been

know - ing, To a wed-ding they're go - ing And for weeks they've been

As Time Goes By

[*Words and music by* HERMAN HUPFELD]

Although Hupfeld's classic was originally written for the 1931 Broadway musical *Everybody's Welcome*, it is best known from the 1942 movie *Casablanca,* which starred Humphrey Bogart and Ingrid Bergman. In the movie it was sung by the relatively obscure Dooley Wilson, but it was a reissued recording by Rudy Vallee that became the hit. A short excerpt of the song appears at the beginning and end of Warner Brothers films.

When Irish Eyes Are Smiling

[*Words by* CHAUNCEY OLCOTT *and* GEORGE GRAFF, JR., *music by* ERNEST BALL]

Published in 1912, this song was written for Olcott's Broadway production of a show called *The Isle O'Dreams*. Olcott specialized in shows about Ireland, and one of his other big hits was *My Wild Irish Rose*. Years later the song was used for the opening of the popular "Duffy's Tavern" radio show. Despite the song's outpouring of positive sentiments towards Ireland, all of the authors were American-born.

Moderate waltz tempo

When I-rish eyes are smil-ing, Sure it's like a morn in spring. In the lilt of I-rish laugh-ter You can

You Made Me Love You

[*Words by* JOSEPH MCCARTHY, *music by* JAMES V. MONACO]

Published in 1913, the song was introduced in the Broadway revue *The Honeymoon Express*. It was immediately recorded by pop idol Al Jolson, whose version remains the best-known rendition of the song. Jolson also performed it in 1946 on the soundtrack of the biopic *The Jolson Story*. Other movie performances of the song were done by Judy Garland and Doris Day. Sometimes the phrase "I didn't want to do it" is added to the title of the song.

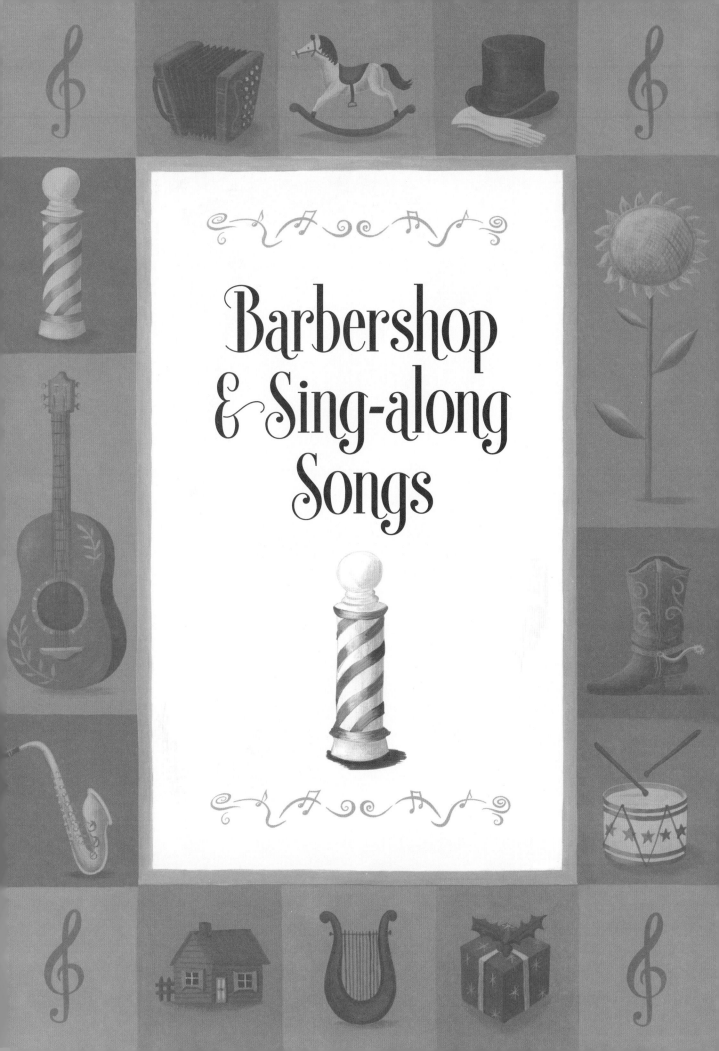

Barbershop & Sing-along Songs

After the Ball

[*Words and music by* CHARLES K. HARRIS]

Within the first months of its publication in 1892, "After the Ball" sold more than 400,000 copies of sheet music. Harris was a banjoist and pianist who had developed a knack for writing "hooks" that pulled the listener into the song. When John Philip Sousa played the tune at the 1893 World Columbian Exposition in Chicago, sales skyrocketed to five million copies.

Gracefully

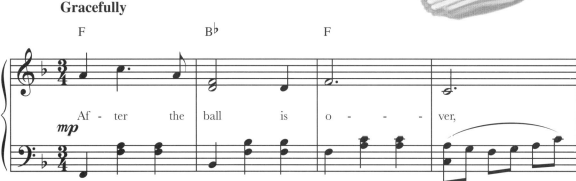

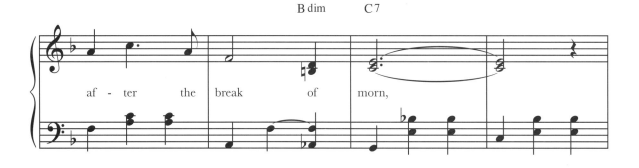

A Bicycle Built for Two

DAISY BELL

[*Words and music by* HARRY DACRE]

Dacre was a British songwriter and initially this song, written in 1892, was successful in London music hall performances. Tony Pastor was the first artist to perform "Daisy Bell" in the United States, and the song initiated a waltz craze in this country, as well as served as a stimulant for many other songs written about bicycles.

Waltz tempo

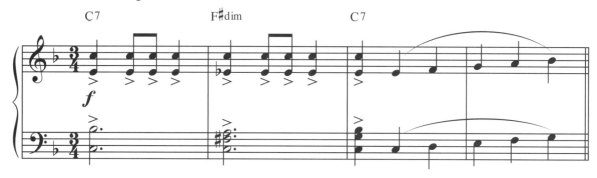

Dai - sy, Dai - sy, give me your

an - swer, do, I'm half

The Band Played On

[*Words by* JOHN F. PALMER, *music by* CHARLES B. WARD]

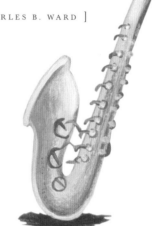

Published in 1895, the sheet music to this song included a dedication to the newspaper the *New York Sunday World*, which was a smart publicity stunt since the newspaper later published the lyrics to the song. The song's description of rapturous and salacious conduct all works out for the best when Casey "marries the girl with the strawberry curl."

Moderate waltz tempo

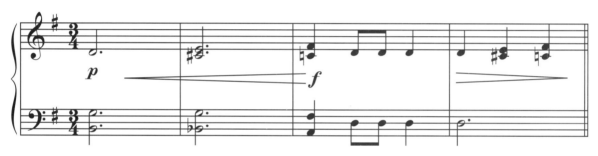

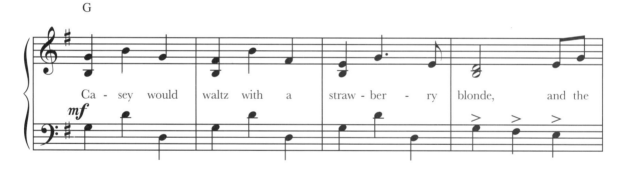

Ca - sey would waltz with a straw - ber - ry blonde, and the

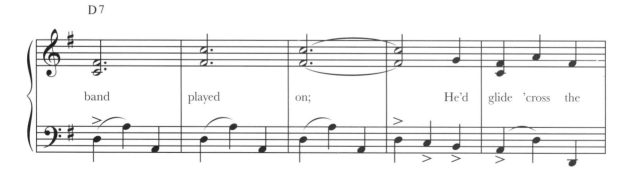

band played on; He'd glide 'cross the

By the Light of the Silvery Moon

[*Words and music by* GUS EDWARDS]

During the vaudeville era, it was not unusual for songwriters to sit in the balcony of a theater and shout out requests for the songs that they had either written or published. Edwards was one of these so-called songpluggers, plying his wares in theaters, saloons, and ferryboats. Edwards wrote this song in 1909, and, in 1953, Doris Day starred in a musical film of the same name.

Moderate soft-shoe tempo

By the light of the sil-ver-y moon,

I want to spoon, to my hon-ey I'll

croon love's tune. Hon-ey-moon,

keep a-shin-ing in June; Your sil - v'ry

beams will bring love dreams, We'll be cud - dl-ing soon

by the sil - ver-y moon.

Carry Me Back to Old Virginny

[*Words and music by* JAMES BLAND,
new words and music by DICK WEISSMAN *and* DAN FOX]

This sentimental tribute to the ways of the old South was written by African-American minstrel performer and composer James Bland in 1880. The original lyrics featured an ex-slave's nostalgic recollections of his old plantation. Because of the sentimental references to "old Massa" and the description of a slave being free from all sorrow, the song is somewhat controversial today. We have modernized the lyrics to reflect contemporary usage.

Slowly

Carry me back to old Virginny,
That's where the cotton and the corn and 'ta - toes grow.
There's where the birds warble sweet in the spring - time;

Paper Doll

[*Words and music by* JOHNNY S. BLACK]

Although "Paper Doll" was written in 1915, it enjoyed its greatest success with a 1943 recording by the Mills Brothers. The brothers were an outstanding vocal quartet, and the song went to the top of the Hit Parade, staying there for more than ten weeks. It can also be heard in the films *The Education of Private Slovik* and *The Majestic,* as well as the British TV show "The Singing Detective."

Moderately slow

I'm gon-na buy a pa-per doll that I can call my own, A

doll that oth-er fel-las can-not steal. And then the

flirt-y, flirt-y guys with their flirt-y, flirt-y eyes Will

Moonlight Bay

[*Words by* EDWARD MADDEN, *music by* PERCY WENRICH]

Wenrich was a talented composer and pianist, playing ragtime as a teenager in Carthage, Missouri, just after the turn of the twentieth century. He later moved to New York City and became a staff songwriter for the Remick Publishing Company. He wrote this song in 1912, and it has been used in many Looney Tunes/Merrie Melodies cartoons and also on Nickelodeon Channel's "Hey Arnold."

In the Good Old Summertime

[*Words by* REN SHIELDS, *music by* GEORGE EVANS]

Initially publishers felt that the title of this song would mean that it would only be sung in the summer months. In 1902, it was published and then featured in the Broadway show *The Defender*. It went on to sell over a million copies of sheet music. Judy Garland starred in a 1951 film featuring the song, and she recorded the tune a few years later for Capitol Records.

Moderate waltz tempo

In the good old sum - mer time, In the

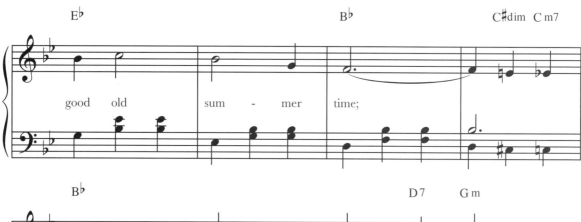

good old sum - mer time;

Stroll - ing through the sha - dy lanes

With your ba - by mine. You hold her hand and she holds yours, And that's a ver - y good sign That she's your toot - sey woot - sey in the good old sum - mer time.

My Bonnie Lies over the Ocean

[TRADITIONAL]

My Bonnie Lies over the Ocean" is a traditional Scottish folk song, possibly dating back to Bonnie Prince Charlie's attempt to restore the Stuarts to the English throne. Fast-forward three hundred years and Tony Sheridan recorded his own arrangement of this song with musical backing by a young and not-yet-famous band called The Beatles. The films *Late Summer Blues* and *Pride and Prejudice* offer even more current performances of the classic tune.

Down by the Old Mill Stream

[*Words and music by* TELL TAYLOR]

Taylor employed a rather odd rhyme scheme in this classic barbershop quartet offering written in 1910. The first line forms a refrain and is the only line of the song that is not rhymed. Just before Taylor's death, he recaptured his inspiration by writing a song that came from the same well; he called it "On the Banks of the Old Mill Stream."

Slowly and somewhat freely

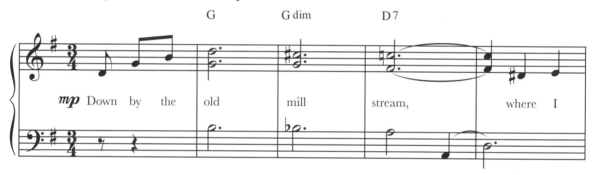

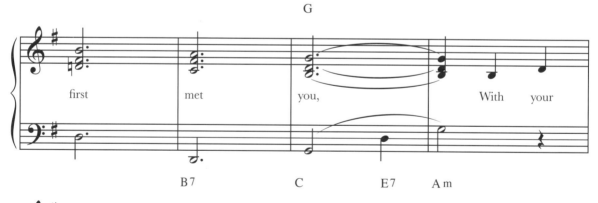

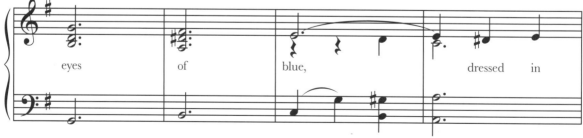

Sweet Adeline

[*Words by* RICHARD H. GERARD, *music by* HARRY ARMSTRONG]

Armstrong wrote this tune in 1896, but it was not published until 1903. His muse was allegedly awakened by a girl who worked at the counter of a New York City department store.

Slowly, and somewhat freely

When You Were Sweet Sixteen

[*Words and music by* JAMES THORNTON]

Written in 1898, this song had already been recorded several times when Al Jolson popularized it in 1929. Perry Como revived the song in 1947, reaching number 2 on the Billboard charts.

Slowly, and rather freely

Take Me Out to the Ball Game

[*Words by* JACK NORWORTH, *music by* ALBERT VON TILZER]

Ironically, neither of the two authors had ever been to a baseball game when they wrote this song. The song was inspired when Norworth viewed a sign at the Polo Grounds baseball field from his vantage point riding the New York City subway in 1908. The song is still used during baseball games in the seventh-inning stretch, even though the song itself is not about someone watching the game; it's about a young woman imploring her beau to take her to a game. Gene Kelly and Frank Sinatra sang the tune in an MGM musical of the same name.

Bright waltz tempo

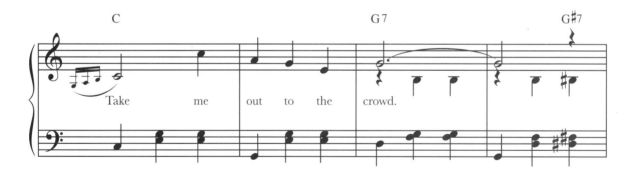

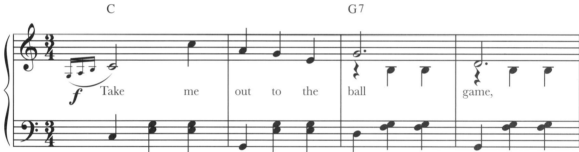

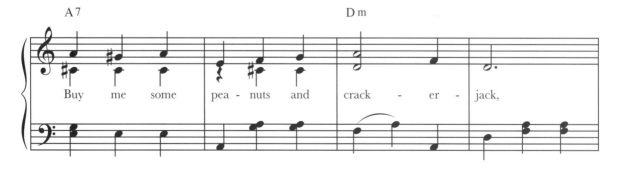

It Ain't Gonna Rain No Mo'

[TRADITIONAL, *new words and music by* DAN FOX]

Ukulele artist Wendall Hall adapted this old folk song, recording it in 1923. Later, Cliff Edwards (Ukulele Ike) and guitarist Nick Lucas performed it as well. The original recording included a short spoken-word section that simulated Hall's stage show. The lyrics are humorous and playful.

Moderately, with spirit

1. It ain't gon-na rain no mo', no mo', It
2. It ain't gon-na rain no mo', no mo', It
3. Well, what did the dev-il say down be-low? It

ain't gon-na rain no mo';
ain't gon-na rain no mo';
ain't gon-na rain no mo';

Come on ev-'ry-
How in the heck can I
Ain't gon-na rain, no it

bod - y now, 'Cause it ain't gon-na rain no mo'.
wash my neck If it ain't gon-na rain no mo'.
ain't gon - na snow, It ain't gon-na rain no mo'.

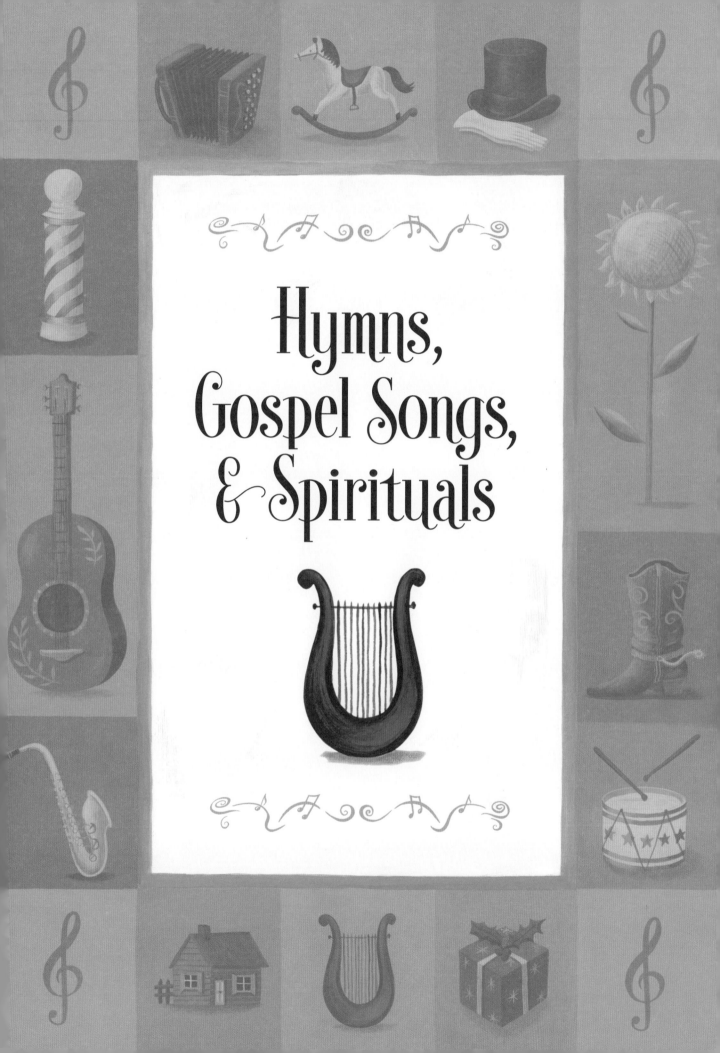

Hymns, Gospel Songs, & Spirituals

Jacob's Ladder

[T R A D I T I O N A L]

The first appearance of this song in print was in the 1867 collection of *Slave Songs of the United States*. There are several versions of this song, which speaks to its popularity.

Amazing Grace

[*Words by* JOHN NEWTON, *music* TRADITIONAL]

Newton wrote the lyrics to "Amazing Grace" in 1749 while experiencing a frightening storm when he was serving on a ship transporting slaves. The source of the melody is in dispute.

Moderately slow

1. A - maz - ing grace, how sweet the sound That
2. 'Twas grace that taught my heart to fear, And
3. Through man - y dan - gers, toils, and snares, I

saved a wretch like me. I
grace my fears re - lieved; How
have al - read - y come; 'Tis

once was lost, but now am found, was
pre - cious did that grace ap - pear The
grace has brought me safe thus far, And

blind but now I see.
hour I first be - lieved.
grace will lead me home.

He's Got the Whole World in His Hands

[TRADITIONAL]

This song is ideally suited for a lead singer and a congregation, with the lead singer laying out each new verse as inspiration strikes. Yet both pop and art singers alike have recorded this stirring hand-clapper. English pop singer Laurie London enjoyed a number 1 hit record with it in 1958. Among the many recorded versions are performances by Leontyne Price, Marian Anderson, Perry Como, Nina Simone, and Odetta.

Moderately, with a strong beat

He's got the whole world in His hands, He's got the whole world in His hands, He's got the whole world

CONTINUE SIMILARLY:

4. He's got uh-you and me, brother, . . .

5. He's got uh-you and me, sister, . . .

6. He's got the rounder and the bounder . . .

7. He's got the whole world . . .

Nobody Knows the Trouble I See

[TRADITIONAL]

In 1867 William Francis Allen, Charles Pickard Ware, and Lucy McKim Garrison compiled a collection called *Slave Songs of the United States.* They printed the words and music of this song, along with a note stating that the song was a favorite in the "colored schools of Charleston" in 1865, and then it spread to the sea islands of Georgia. They also mention receiving another version collected in Florida. Art singers Roland Hayes and Paul Robeson each recorded the song, and supposedly Abraham Lincoln cried when he heard it.

All My Trials

[TRADITIONAL]

Sometimes found under the title "All My Sins Been Taken Away," similar verses collected in 1915 are printed in Newman I. White's book *American Negro Folk-Songs*. During the U.S. Civil Rights Movement of the 1950s and 1960s, folk artists such as Joan Baez, Peter, Paul and Mary, and Pete Seeger recorded it. Elvis Presley used part of it in his "An American Trilogy," and legendary English singer-songwriter Nick Drake recorded it as a duet with his sister Gabrielle. The appeal of this Bahamian lullaby is partly based on its socially egalitarian message.

Moderately and rather freely

mf
1. Now, hush, lit-tle ba-by don't you cry, You
2. If re-lig-ion was a thing that mon-ey could buy, The

know that man was born to die;
rich would live and the poor would die;

p All my trials, Lord, soon be o-ver.

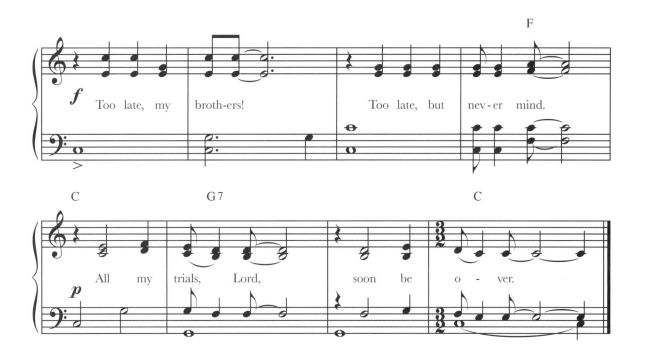

Too late, my broth-ers! Too late, but nev-er mind.

All my trials, Lord, soon be o - ver.

3. I had a little book that was given to me,
   And ev'ry page spelled victory!
   All my trials, Lord,
   Soon be over.

4. The Jordan River is chilly and cold,
   It chills the body but not the soul.
   All my trials, Lord,
   Soon be over.

Simple Gifts

[*Words and music by* ELDER JOSEPH BRACKETT, JR.]

The Shakers were a nineteenth-century New England religious sect. Brackett wrote this hymn in 1848, and although the Shaker communities themselves did not survive into the twentieth century, this melody achieved worldwide fame through its use in American composer Aaron Copland's popular ballet score "Appalachian Spring." Copland's adaptation was used as the theme music for the CBS news when Edward R. Murrow was the anchor. It was also featured in the Broadway show *Blast!* and in the television series "Alias Smith and Jones."

Moderately

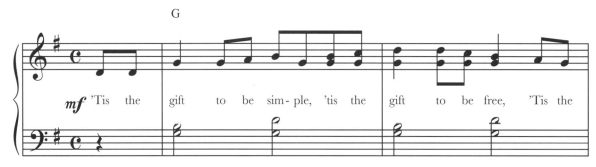

'Tis the gift to be simple, 'tis the gift to be free, 'Tis the

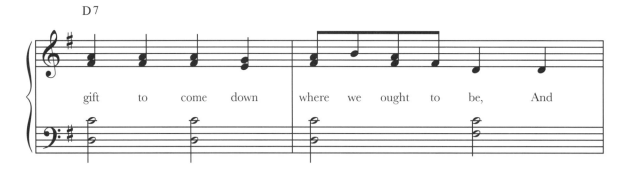

gift to come down where we ought to be, And

when we find our-selves in the place just right, It will

Swing Low, Sweet Chariot

[*Words and music by* WALLIS WILLIS]

It is not widely known that some Native American tribes had African-American slaves. Willis was a Choctaw slave who was inspired to write this song about the River Jordan. After the Civil War, Alexander Reid, a minister at a Choctaw boarding school, heard Willis singing this song and transcribed it. He sent the music to the Jubilee Singers of Fisk University in Nashville. The first recording of the song was by the Standard Quartet in 1894.

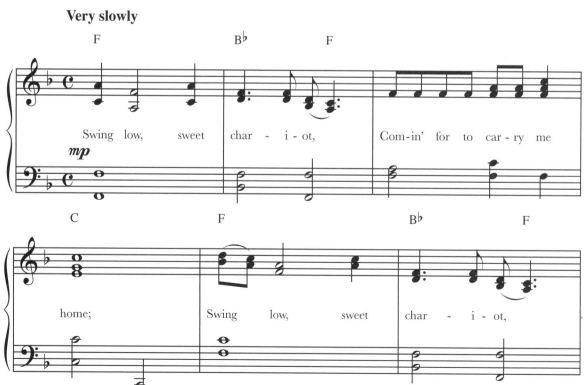

Very slowly

Swing low, sweet char - i - ot, Com-in' for to car - ry me home; Swing low, sweet char - i - ot,

Shall We Gather at the River

[*Words and music by* ROBERT LOWRY]

Composed in 1864, the song was published a year later. Lowry wrote the song on a particularly hot day, envisioning a heavenly river and a gathering of the saints. The song is well known in Baptist congregations. A portion of the song was used in the 1985 award-winning movie *A Trip to Bountiful*. It was sung at the funeral of Supreme Court justice and civil liberties scholar William O. Douglas.

Not too fast, with a steady beat

Joshua Fit the Battle

[TRADITIONAL]

Joshua was Moses's successor, and this impassioned song describes his conquest of Jericho. Joshua was the leader of recently freed slaves who defeated the better equipped army of the Philistines. This song contains what scholars have described as a "coded message." On the plantation, the slave owner might accept the lyrics as being historical, but to the slaves, it described their impending liberation.

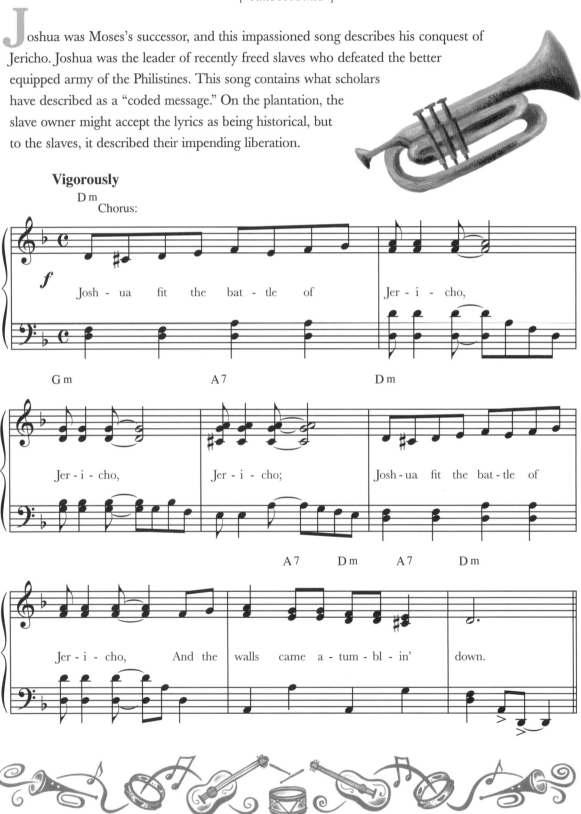

Vigorously

Josh - ua fit the bat - tle of Jer - i - cho, Jer - i - cho, Jer - i - cho; Josh - ua fit the bat - tle of Jer - i - cho, And the walls came a - tum - bl - in' down.

This Little Light of Mine

[TRADITIONAL]

A staple of the U.S. Civil Rights Movement, this song appears in the *Sing for Freedom* collection edited by Guy and Candie Carawan. The light mentioned in the song is the light of freedom and love, and the song leader improvises the names of towns where the light needs to shine, as in "Down in Mississippi, we're going to let it shine." A book by Kay Mills about Fannie Lou Hamer, the black leader of the Mississippi Freedom Party, uses this title.

Bright gospel beat

1. This lit-tle light of mine, I'm a-gon-na let it shine;
2. I've got the light of grace, I'm a-gon-na let it shine;
3. We've got the light of love, We're a-gon-na let it shine;

When the Saints Go Marching In

[TRADITIONAL]

Also known as "The Saints," this upbeat song has existed in two very different incarnations. On one level, it is a spiritual that is sung in church. The other common usage is as a Dixieland jazz standard, played by dozens of combos in New Orleans and elsewhere. Louis Armstrong made a popular recording of the song in the 1930s, and Judy Garland, Fats Domino, Jerry Lee Lewis, and many others have recorded it. It is so omnipresent that a sign at Preservation Hall, the traditional jazz headquarters in New Orleans, announces that requests for "Saints" cost $5!

Gimme That Old Time Religion

[TRADITIONAL]

Newman I. White traced this song to Southern white camp meetings in North Carolina in 1875. Various scholars dispute whether spirituals originated in hymns of African Americans or white singers. "Gimme That Old Time Religion" appears in various hymnbooks and collections of songs sung by both white and black singers. In some of the versions collected from African Americans, there are references to joining the Union band or the Union–presumably this refers to the Civil War.

Moderately, with spirit

Chorus:

f Gim-me that old - time re - li - gion, Gim-me that old - time re-li - gion, Gim-me that old - time re - li - gion; It's good e-nough for me.

Verses:

1. It was good for the He - brew chil - dren, It was
2. It will car - ry us up to heav - en, It will

Rock of Ages

[*Words by* REVEREND AUGUSTUS MONTAGU TOPLADY, *music by* THOMAS HASTINGS]

The first publication of the lyrics to this hymn occurred in *The Gospel Magazine* in 1775. The music was added around 1830. Supposedly the song was inspired when Reverend Toplady was caught in a storm and found shelter in a gap in a gorge.

1. Rock of Ages, cleft for me, Let me hide myself in Thee. Let the water and the blood From Thy wounded side which flowed Be of sin the double cure: Save from wrath and make me pure.

2. Could my tears forever flow? Could my zeal no languor know. These for sin could not atone; Thou must save and Thou alone. In my hand no price I bring, Simply to Thy cross I cling.

3. While I draw this fleeting breath, When my eyes shall close in death, When I rise to worlds unknown And behold Thee on Thy throne. Rock of Ages, cleft for me, Let me hide myself in Thee.

Christmas & Other Holiday Songs

The First Noël

[TRADITIONAL]

Noël is the French term for Christmas, but this traditional holiday song is of English origin. "The First Noël" was most likely written in the sixteenth or seventeenth centuries. It was first published in *Some Ancient Christmas Carols* in 1823 and *Gilbert and Sandys Christmas Carols* in 1833, which was edited by William Sandys and arranged and edited by Davies Gilvert. This popular carol has been recorded by a diverse group of artists, including The Supremes and Whitney Houston.

3. This star drew nigh to the northwest;
   O'er Bethlehem it took its rest,
   And there it did both stop and stay,
   Right o'er the place where Jesus lay.
   (repeat chorus)

4. Then entered in there Wise Men three,
   Fall rev'rently upon their knee,
   And offered there in His presence
   Their gold and myrrh and frankincense.
   (repeat chorus)

Adeste Fideles

O COME ALL YE FAITHFUL

[*English words by* FREDERICK OAKELEY, *Latin words and music by* JOHN FRANCIS WADE]

John Francis Wade, an eighteen-century Englishman who lived and worked in France, seems to have been the author of both the Latin words and the music of this famous hymn. But some authorities trace the origins of the music to earlier French circle dances that were popular in the 1740s. Sailors probably brought the song to America, and the first edition bears the subtitle "The Favorite Portuguez [sic] Hymn on the Nativity." The translation was written in 1852 by Frederick Oakeley, a Catholic priest who became Canon of Westminster.

Majestically

2. Sing, choirs of angels,
   Sing in exultation,
   Sing all ye citizens of heav'n above.
   Glory to God, all glory in the highest.
   O come let us adore Him,
   O come let us adore Him,
   O come let us adore Him,
   Christ, the Lord.

3. Yea, Lord, we greet Thee,
   Born this happy morning,
   Jesus, to Thee be glory giv'n;
   Word of the Father, now in flesh appearing:
   O come let us adore Him,
   O come let us adore Him,
   O come let us adore Him,
   Christ, the Lord.

Silent Night

[*English words adapted from the German by* JOSEPH MOHR, *music by* FRANZ GRUBER]

This song was first performed Christmas 1818, in Oberndorf, Austria. From that first performance until today, the simple melody and heartfelt words have made "Silent Night" a Christmas favorite.

Deck the Hall

[TRADITIONAL]

This Welsh melody has been sung with a number of different lyrics. This version of the song was not published in America until 1881, almost a hundred years after its first publication in Britain.

Joy to the World

[*Words by* ISAAC WATTS, *music by* LOWELL MASON]

Because some of the melodic fragments in this famous work resemble music from George Frederick Handel's *Messiah*, Lowell Mason originally credited his idol as composer of "Joy to the World." Modern authorities, however, generally credit Mason as the composer. The composer of the words, Isaac Watts, is known as "the father of English hymnody."

Majestically, with spirit

1. Joy to the world! The Lord is come! Let earth re- ceive her King. Let ev- 'ry heart pre- pare Him
2. Joy to the earth! The Sav- ior reigns; Let men their songs em- ploy: While fields and floods, rocks, hills and
3. He rules the world with truth and grace; And makes the na- tions prove The glo- ries of His right- eous

We Three Kings

[*Words and music by* JOHN HENRY HOPKINS]

Written for an 1857 Christmas pageant by American minister John Henry Hopkins, "We Three Kings" tells the story of the three wise men who come to Bethlehem to worship baby Jesus.

Moderately

4. Balthasar:
   Myrrh is mine, its bitter perfume
   Breathes a life of gathering doom;
   Sorrowing, sighing, bleeding, dying,
   Sealed in the stone-cold tomb. O
   (repeat chorus)

5. All:
   Glorious now, behold Him arise,
   King and God and Sacrifice;
   Alleluia, alleluia!
   Sounds through the earth and skies. O
   (repeat chorus)

Jingle Bells

[*Words and music by* JAMES PIERPONT]

When is a Christmas song not a Christmas song? "Jingle Bells" was written originally as a Thanksgiving song for a Sunday School class by an uncle of the financier J. P. Morgan. The song never mentions Christmas, New Year's, Mary, or Jesus. Nevertheless, the "jingle bell" rhythm–suggestive of sleigh bells in the snow–proved irresistible, and helped the song become one of the best-known Christmas songs of all time.

Gaily

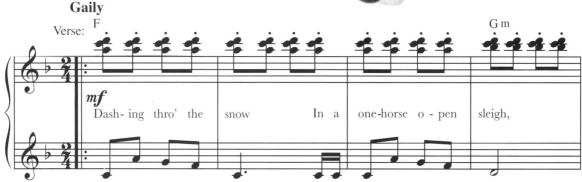

Verse: Dash- ing thro' the snow In a one-horse o - pen sleigh,

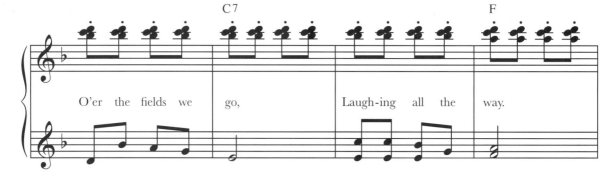

O'er the fields we go, Laugh-ing all the way.

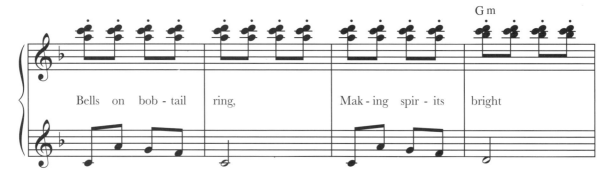

Bells on bob - tail ring, Mak-ing spir - its bright

God Rest Ye Merry, Gentlemen

[TRADITIONAL]

Although no one has been able to trace this carol to its source, there are hints in the music that it is very old. Most music composed since about the seventeenth century is written in major or minor keys, but this tune seems to come from an earlier time when ancient church modes were still in use. Ebenezer Scrooge, as portrayed in Charles Dickens's *A Christmas Carol*, gets angry when he hears this carol being sung in the street. First published in 1827, the song would have been well-known in Dickens's London, where it was popular with the street singers of the day.

save us all from Satan's pow'r When we were gone a - stray:
which His moth - er Mar - y did noth - ing take in scorn:
that in Beth - le - hem was born the Son of God by name:

Chorus:
O tid - ings of com - fort and joy, com - fort and joy! O

tid - ings of com - fort and joy.

after last chorus only

4. "Fear not," then said the angel,
   "Let nothing you affright,
   This day is born a Savior
   Of a pure Virgin bright,
   To free all those who trust in Him
   From Satan's pow'r and might,"
   (repeat chorus)

5. The shepherds at those tidings
   Rejoicèd much in mind,
   And left their flocks a-feeding
   In tempest, storm and wind,
   And went to Bethlehem straightaway
   This blessèd Babe to find:
   (repeat chorus)

6. But when to Bethlehem they came,
   Whereat this Infant lay,
   They found Him in a manger
   Where oxen feed on hay;
   His mother Mary kneeling,
   Unto the Lord did pray:
   (repeat chorus)

7. Now to the Lord sing praises
   All you within this place,
   And with true love and brotherhood
   Each other now embrace;
   This holy tide of Christmas
   All others doth deface:
   (repeat chorus)

The Twelve Days of Christmas

[TRADITIONAL]

Although this well-known "cumulative" carol seems like a simple catalog of gifts, its true significance lies much deeper. The partridge, a bird ready to die to defend its young, represents Jesus and two turtledoves represent Mary and Joseph.

Gaily

Use this music for the 6th through the 12th day

CONTINUE SIMILARLY:

7. On the seventh day . . . seven swans a-swimming,
8. On the eighth day . . . eight maids a-milking,
9. On the ninth day . . . nine ladies dancing,
10. On the tenth day . . . ten lords a-leaping,
11. On the eleventh day . . . eleven pipers piping,
12. On the twelfth day . . . twelve drummers drumming,

We Gather Together

[*Words by* DR. THEODORE BAKER, *music* DUTCH FOLK TUNE]

The music of this song is likely a Dutch folk tune, although some credit the melody to one of two obscure seventeenth-century Dutch composers, Adrianus Valerius or Edward Kremser.

O Little Town of Bethlehem

[*Words by* PHILLIPS BROOKS, *music by* LEWIS H. REDNER]

Phillips Brooks was an Episcopalian minister who traveled to Jerusalem during the final year of the American Civil War. Brooks was deeply moved by the experience and a few years later wrote the words of "O Little Town of Bethlehem," which he first intended as a children's hymn. The organist in Brooks's church was Lewis H. Redner, who set the words to music in time for Christmas of 1868.

1. O lit - tle town of Beth - le - hem, How still we see thee lie! A - bove thy deep and dream - less sleep The si - lent stars go by. Yet

2. For Christ is born of Mar - y, And gath - ered all a - bove, While mor - tals sleep, the an - gels keep Their watch of won - d'ring love. O

3. How si - lent - ly, how si - lent - ly The won - drous gift is giv'n! So God im - parts to hu - man hearts The bless - ings of His heav'n. No

4. Where children pure and happy
   Pray to the blessèd Child,
   Where misery cries out to Thee,
   Son of the mother mild;
   Where charity stands watching
   And faith holds wide the door,
   The dark night wakes, the glory breaks
   And Christmas comes once more.

5. O holy Child of Bethlehem
   Descend on us, we pray;
   Cast out our sin and enter in,
   Be born in us today.
   We hear the Christmas angels,
   The great glad tidings tell:
   O come to us, abide with us,
   Our Lord, Immanuel.

The Dreidel Song

[*Words* ANONYMOUS, *music* YIDDISH FOLK TUNE]

A tradition associated with Hannukah is the spinning of a clay top called a *dreidel*. Depending on where the top comes to rest, players either put something into a pot or win something from it.

Happily, with spirit

1. I have a lit - tle drei-del, I made it out of clay And when it's dry and read - y The drei - del I shall play. Oh, drei - del, drei - del, drei-del, I made it out of clay. Oh, drei - del, drei - del, drei-del, Then drei - del I shall play.

2. It has a love - ly bod - y With legs so short and thin; And when it is all tired It drops and then I win. Oh, drei - del, drei - del, drei-del, With legs so short and thin; Oh, drei - del, drei - del, drei-del, It drops and then I win.

3. My drei-del's al - ways play-ful, It loves to dance and spin; A hap - py game of drei-del, Come play, now let's be - gin. Oh, drei - del, drei - del, drei-del, It loves to dance and spin; Oh, drei - del, drei - del, drei-del, Come play, now let's be - gin.

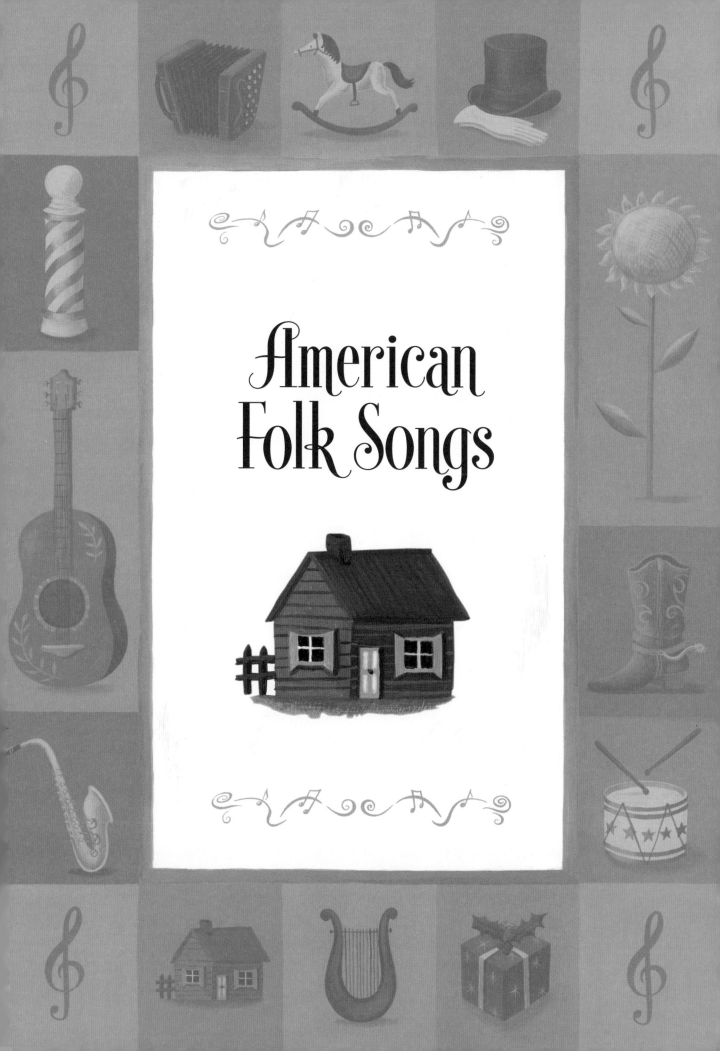

American Folk Songs

Aura Lea

[*Words by* WILLIAM FOSDICK, *music by* R. POULTON]

This song was published originally in 1861, with a dedication to S. C. Campbell of Hooley and Campbell's Minstrels. Elvis Presley enjoyed a major hit with his recording of this tune, using a different set of lyrics credited to him and Vera Matson. His version was called "Love Me Tender."

Moderately slow

Shortnin' Bread

[TRADITIONAL]

Folklorist Dorothy Scarborough collected a version of this song and printed it in her book *On the Trail of Negro Folk Songs,* which was published in 1925. The title refers to any type of Southern quick bread that incorporates shortening and flour.

The Blue-Tail Fly

JIMMIE CRACK CORN

[AUTHOR UNKNOWN]

It is not clear who wrote this song, although some early editions credit Dan Emmett as its author. "The Blue-Tail Fly" was performed by the Virginia Minstrels, and F. D. Bentee published the song in 1846, two years after the troupe had disbanded. Some scholars believe that the melody is an African-American tune that was reworked by white minstrels. Burl Ives popularized the song through recordings and performances, and many other artists have recorded it, including Pete Seeger, bluesman Big Bill Broonzy, and Bugs Bunny in the Warner Brothers cartoon *Lumber Jack-Rabbit*.

Moderately fast

Verses: *freely*

1. When I was young I used to wait On
2. And when he rides in the af - ter - noon, I'd
3. One day he ride a - round the farm, The

mas - ter and give him his plate, And pass the bot - tle when
fol - low with a hick - 'ry broom, The po - ny, he was
flies so num - 'rous they did swarm, One chanced to bite him

a tempo

he got dry, And brush a - way the blue - tail fly.
like to shy, When bit - ten by the blue - tail fly.
on the thigh; The dev - il take the blue - tail fly.

Chorus:

F   C7   F

Jim-mie crack corn and I don't care, Jim-mie crack corn and I don't care,

F7   B♭   C7   F

Jim-mie crack corn and I don't care, My mas-ter's gone a - way.

4. The pony run, he jump, he pitch,
   And threw old master in the ditch,
   He died; the jury wondered why:
   The verdict was "The blue-tail fly."
   (repeat chorus)

5. They laid him under a 'simmon tree,
   His epitaph is there to see;
   "Beneath this stone I'm forced to lie,
   A victim of the blue-tail fly."
   (repeat chorus)

Shenandoah

[TRADITIONAL]

This romantic ballad, presumably sung by a white riverboat man, asks an Indian chief to allow the singer to take him across the wide Missouri River to see the Indian chief's daughter. The song was reportedly popular with riverboat men who plied the Mississippi and Missouri Rivers and oceangoing sailors as well. Shenandoah is also the name of a Virginia river.

Very freely throughout

CONTINUE SIMILARLY:

4. Oh, Shenandoah's my native valley...

5. Oh, Shenandoah, I'll never leave you...

6. Oh, Shenandoah, I long to hear you...

Buttermilk Hill

[TRADITIONAL]

Some scholars believe the origin of this tune goes back to seventeenth-century Ireland, when the Irish fought unsuccessfully for King James II against the French. Others date the song from the American Revolution and give it a different name. The song is a lament sung by a soldier's lady friend, reflecting her concern about his military service.

Slowly

1. Oh, here I sit on But-ter-milk Hill; Who can blame me cry'n' my fill? And ev-'ry tear would turn a mill:
2. Oh, me, oh my, I loved him so; Broke my heart to see him go. And on-ly time will heal my woe:
3. I'll sell my rod and sell my reel; Like-wise I'll sell my spin-ning wheel And buy my love a sword of steel:

John-ny has gone for a sol-dier.

I've Been Working on the Railroad

[TRADITIONAL]

In 1894 this modern version of "I've Been Working on the Railroad" was printed in a book of songs sung at Princeton University. It was titled "Levee Song," and the rather racist lyrics were printed in dialect. The University of Texas football fight song "The Eyes of Texas" uses the tune with another set of lyrics.

Moderate steady beat

Strum each chord lightly, like a guitar

I've been work-ing on the rail - road all the live - long

day; I've been work-ing on the rail - road just to

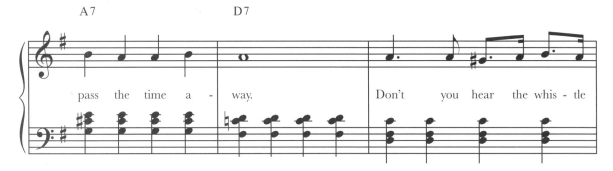

pass the time a - way. Don't you hear the whis - tle

Someone's in the Kitchen with Dinah

[TRADITIONAL]

An English firm published this song in the 1830s or 1840s crediting H. Cave as the composer. The original title used was "Old Joe, Somebody in the House with Dinah." Dinah was a generic name for an enslaved African-American woman. E. P. Christy, the leader of the Christy Minstrels, used a similar melody for his tune "Good Night Ladies," published in 1847.

Moderately, with a steady beat

Some - one's in the kitch - en with Di - nah,

Some - one's in the kitch - en, I know - ow - ow - ow;

Some - one's in the kitch - en with Di - nah,

Strum - min' on the old ban - jo. He's strum - min':

Fee - - fi fid - dle - e - i - o,

Fee - fi - fid - dle - e - i o - o - o - o;

Fee - - fi fid - dle - e - i - o,

Strum - min' on the old ban - jo.

On Top of Old Smoky

[TRADITIONAL]

In 1951, the Weavers, assisted by Terry Gilkyson, had a number 1 hit with this Appalachian folk song. Many verses of "Old Smoky" are found in other traditional mountain songs.

Down in the Valley

[TRADITIONAL]

A beautiful and often-recorded love song, "Down in the Valley" has been performed with many sets of lyrics. The names and places change in each version, but the sentiment remains the same.

Moderately

1. Down in the valley, valley so low, Late in the
2. Roses love sunshine, violets love dew; Angels in
3. If you don't love me, love who you please; Throw your arms

evening hear the wind blow.
heaven know I love you.
'round me, give my heart ease.

Hear the wind blow, love, hear the wind blow; Late in the
Know I love you, dear, know I love you; Angels in
Give my heart ease, love, give my heart ease; Throw your arms

1, 2. G   **3.** G

evening hear the wind blow.
heaven know I love you.
'round me, give my heart ease.

Poor Wayfaring Stranger

[TRADITIONAL]

Folksinger and actor Burl Ives based his performing persona on the title of this song, calling himself "the wayfaring stranger," a title he used for his autobiography as well. Ives recorded it in 1944 on his album of the same name. The song is clearly a gospel song, the origins of which have been variously attributed to Ireland or to an African-American spiritual.

Slowly

there ... to meet my Sav-ior, I'm go-ing there ... to see my

Lord; I'm on-ly go — ing o-ver Jor-dan, I'm on-ly

go — ing o-ver home. I'm on-ly go — ing o-ver home.

Camptown Races

[*Words and music by* STEPHEN FOSTER]

Stephen Foster wrote this song in 1850 for the famous Christy Minstrels. Christy was so enamored of Foster's work that his group sang Foster's songs even before they were published. The song depicts a horse race and includes a colorful description of the race and of gamblers betting on the various horses.

3. Old muley cow come on to the track,
   Doodah! Doodah!
   The bob-tail fling her over his back,
   Oh, doodah day.
   Then fly along like a railroad car,
   Doodah! Doodah!
   Runnin' a race wit' a shootin' star,
   Oh, doodah day.
   (repeat chorus)

4. See them flyin' on a ten-mile heat,
   Doodah! Doodah!
   Round the racetrack, then repeat,
   Oh, doodah day.
   I win my money on the bob-tail nag,
   Doodah! Doodah!
   I keep my money in an old tow-bag,
   Oh, doodah day.
   (repeat chorus)

Old Folks at Home

WAY DOWN UPON THE SWANEE RIVER

[*Words and music by* STEPHEN FOSTER]

E. P. Christy's name appeared under the original composer credits for this song, but Foster was the actual composer. He battled poverty during his entire adult life, but this song proved to be his most successful, from the standpoint of royalties that he earned through the sale of hundreds of thousands of copies of the sheet music. Several years later, songwriting superstar Irving Berlin tipped his hat to Foster in the song "Alexander's Ragtime Band," when he quoted the song in ragtime style. In 1935, the state of Florida adopted "Old Folks at Home" as its official state song.

Moderately slow (without dragging)

Verses:

1. Way down up-on the Swa-nee Riv-er, Far, far a-way,
2. All 'round the lit-tle farm I wan-dered When I was young.

There's where my heart is turn-ing ev-er, There's where the old folks stay.
Then man-y hap-py days I squan-dered, Man-y the songs I sung.

All up and down the
When will I see the

Erie Canal

[TRADITIONAL]

Construction of the Erie Canal was an ambitious project that lasted from 1817 to 1825. Folklorist John Lomax found a complaint filed against Erie Canal boatmen by irate townspeople who complained about their loud singing. It was the singing that helped the workers get through their monotonous duties. Another version of this song, using a different melody and lacking the bridge, was collected by a number of folklorists, including Carl Sandburg.

Moderately

I've got a mule and her name is Sal; Fif-teen miles on the E-rie Ca-nal. She's a good old work-er and a good old pal; Fif-teen miles on the E-rie Ca-nal. We've hauled some barg-es

Banks of the Ohio

[TRADITIONAL]

Nineteenth-century folk musicians sang a number of ballads about murdered girls. Songs such as "Pretty Polly," "Down in the Willow Garden," and "Naomi Wise," like "Banks of the Ohio," all concern girls who are murdered by their boyfriends. Sometimes this violence is a product of a failed love affair; in other cases, the girls have become pregnant. This was one of the first songs that Joan Baez recorded, and subsequent artists who have recorded the song include country artists Charley Pride, Olivia Newton-John, and Bill Monroe.

Moderately

Verses:

1. I asked my love to take a walk, Just to walk a lit-tle way. And as we walked a-long we talked
2. I held a knife close to her breast, Close-ly to her bos-om pressed. "Oh, Wil-lie dear, don't mur-der me;
3. Re-turn-ing home 'tween twelve and one, Think-ing of the deed I done, I killed the on - - - ly girl I loved

All a - bout
our wed - ding day.

I'm un - pre - pared
for e - ter - ni - ty."

Be - cause she would
not be my bride.

Chorus:

And on - ly say
that you'll be mine,

In our home
we'll hap - py be.

Out be -

side
where the wa - ters flow

Down by the

banks
of the O - hi - o.

215

The Yellow Rose of Texas

[TRADITIONAL]

The Yellow Rose of Texas" was published in 1858. The original song portrayed a free mulatto woman named Emily D. West, who was seized by Mexican soldiers during the looting of Galveston.

Moderately

1. There's a yel- low rose in Tex- as that I am goin' to see; No oth- er fel- ler knows her, no fel- ler, on- ly me. She cried so when I left her, it like to broke my heart, And if I ev- er find her we nev- er more will part.

2. Where the Ri- o Grande is flow-ing, and the star- ry skies are bright, She walks a- long the riv- er in the qui- et sum- mer night. I know that she re- mem- bers when we part- ed long a- go, I prom- ised to come back a- gain, and not to leave her so.

3. Oh, now I'm goin' to find her, for my heart is full of woe,
   We'll sing the song together that we sung so long ago.
   We'll play the banjo gaily, and we'll sing the songs of yore,
   And the yellow rose of Texas will be mine forever more.
   (repeat chorus)

If I Had a Hammer

THE HAMMER SONG

[*Words and music by* LEE HAYS *and* PETE SEEGER]

Hays and Seeger first wrote this song in 1949, and their vocal group, The Weavers, recorded it the same year on the Hootenanny label. Peter, Paul and Mary made it into a top ten hit in 1962 with an impassioned performance. The song became one of the anthems of the U.S. Civil Rights Movement, and many other artists recorded it as well.

Moderate steady beat

1. If I had a ham - mer, I'd ham-mer in the morn - ing, I'd ham-mer in the eve - ning, all o - ver this land. I'd ham-mer out

2. If I had a bell, I'd ring it in the morn - ing, I'd ring it in the eve - ning, all o - ver this land. I'd ring out

3. If I had a song,
   I'd sing it in the morning,
   I'd sing it in the evening all over this land.
   I'd sing out danger,
   I'd sing out a warning,
   I'd sing out love between
   my brothers and my sisters
   All over this land.

4. Well, I've got a hammer,
   And I've got a bell,
   And I've got a song all over this land.
   It's the hammer of justice,
   It's the bell of freedom,
   It's the song about love between
   my brothers and my sisters
   All over this land.

Tom Dooley

[*Words and music, collected, adapted, and arranged by* FRANK WARNER,
JOHN A. LOMAX, *and* ALAN LOMAX *from the singing of* FRANK PROFITT]

Frank Profitt, of Wilkes County, North Carolina, sang this song for folklorist Frank Warner in 1938. Profitt had learned the song from his father. It was based on a true story of a romance that went bad between Tom Dula and Laura Foster. Dula was hanged in 1868, after two trials. In 1958, the Kingston Trio's recording of "Tom Dooley" used a monologue in the opening section of the recording. The disc sold over six million copies and sparked the folk music revival in the United States.

there   I   took   her   life,   I   met   her   on   the
Reck - on   where   I'll   be?   If   it   had - na   been   for
Reck - on   where   I'll   be?   In   some   lone - some

moun - tain   And   stabbed   her   with   my   knife.
Gray - son   I'd - a   been   in   Ten - nes - see.
val - ley   A -   hang - in'   on   a   white   oak   tree.

Chorus:

Hang   down   your   head,   Tom   Doo - ley,

mf

Hang   down   your   head   and   cry;   Hang   down   your   head,   Tom

Doo - ley,   Poor   boy,   you're   bound   to   die.

Goodnight, Irene

[*Words and music by* HUDDIE LEDBETTER (LEADBELLY) *and* JOHN A. LOMAX]

Leadbelly first heard this song from his uncle, and verses of it can be found in several collections of African-American songs published during the 1920s. Blues scholar Paul Oliver traced it to an 1886 pop song by Gussie Davis. However, it was Leadbelly's arrangement of the song that the Weavers rearranged for their huge hit record of 1950. That recording stayed on the charts at number 1 for ten weeks. Everyone from Brian Wilson, to Van Morrison, Tom Waits, Chet Atkins, Gene Autry, Johnny Cash, Frank Sinatra, Les Paul, and many more have recorded it.

Moderate waltz tempo

Oh, Them Golden Slippers!

[*Words and music by* JAMES BLAND]

James Bland was one of the most famous minstrel composers and was one of the few who actually was an African American. Bland graduated from Howard University in Washington, D.C., at the age of nineteen, and he was also a page at the U.S. House of Representatives. After initially suffering severe difficulties in finding employment in white minstrel companies, Bland joined Jack Harvey's all-black troupe in 1881. He wrote "Golden Slippers" in 1879, using dialect that has been edited in more modern printings of the song. He got the idea for the song from a spiritual sung by the Fisk Jubilee Singers. The catchy tune is also played today as a fiddle or banjo instrumental piece.

Brightly, with spirit

G

mf

1. Oh, my   gold - en   slip - pers are   laid   a - way,   'Cause I
2. Oh, my   old   ban - jo,   it's hang - in'   on   the   wall,   'Cause it
3. So   it's   good - bye   chil - dren,   I will   have   to   go,   Where the

D 7

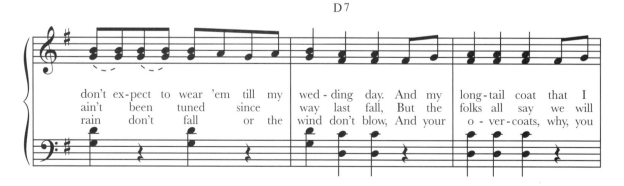

don't ex - pect to wear 'em till my   wed - ding day. And my   long - tail coat that I
ain't   been   tuned   since   way last fall, But the   folks all   say   we will
rain   don't   fall   or   the   wind don't blow, And your   o - ver - coats, why, you

G

loved so well, I will wear up in the cha-riot in the morn; And my
have a good time When we ride up in the cha-riot in the morn. There's ol'
will not need, When you ride up in the cha-riot in the morn. But your

G

long white robe that I bought last June, I'm a
Broth - er Ben and Sis - ter Luce, They will
gold - en slip - pers must be nice and clean, And your

D 7

gon - na get it changed 'cause it fits too soon, And the
te - le - graph the news to Un - cle 'bac - co Juice; What a
age must be a - just - a sweet six - teen; And your

old gray hoss that I used to drive, I will
great camp meet'n there will be that day When we
white kid gloves you will have to wear When you

G

hitch him to the cha - riot in the morn.
ride up in the cha - riot in the morn.
ride up in the cha - riot in the morn.

The Wreck of the Edmund Fitzgerald

[*Words and music by* GORDON LIGHTFOOT]

In 1975, the ship S.S. *Edmund Fitzgerald* sank in Lake Superior. A year later Gordon Lightfoot recorded this song, paying tribute to the lost sailors. The lyrics faithfully describe the ship, its captain, and the gale warnings that were issued by the National Weather Service. Lightfoot's song is one of the few that has ever become a hit with only a single verse melody and no chorus. In this way the song resembles a traditional English folk song.

Brightly

mf 1. The (2. The) leg-end lives on from the Chip-pe-wa on down Of the ship was the pride of the A-mer-i-can side, Com-ing

big lake they called "Git-chee Gu-mee." back from some mill in Wis-con-sin.

The lake, it is said, nev-er gives up her As the big freight-ers go it was big-ger than

G   D   Asus2

chewed   When the   gales   of   No -   vem - ber   came   ear - ly.
Could it   be   the   north   wind they'd   been   feel - in'?

For repeats   Fine

2. The

3. The wind in the wires
   made a tattletale sound
   And a wave broke over the railing.
   And every man knew,
   as the captain did, too,
   T'was the Witch of November come stealin'.
   The dawn came late
   and the breakfast had to wait
   When the gales of November came slashin'.
   When afternoon came
   it was freezin' rain
   In the face of a hurricane west wind.

4. When suppertime came,
   the old cook came on deck sayin'
   "Fellas, it's too rough to feed ya."
   At seven P.M.
   a main hatchway caved in,
   He said, "Fellas, it's been good to know ya."
   The captain wired in
   he had water comin' in
   And the good ship and crew was in peril.
   And later that night
   when his lights went outta sight
   Came the wreck of the Edmund Fitzgerald.

5. Does anyone know where the love of God goes
   When the waves turn the minutes to hours?
   The searchers all say
   they'd have made Whitefish Bay
   If they'd put fifteen more miles behind her.
   They might have split up
   or they might have capsized
   They may have broke deep and took water.
   And all that remains is the faces and the names
   Of the wives and the sons and the daughters.

6. In a musty old hall in Detroit, they prayed
   In the maritime sailors' cathedral.
   The church bell chimed
   till it rang twenty-nine times
   For each man on the Edmund Fitzgerald.
   The legend lives on
   from the Chippewa on down
   Of the big lake they call "Gitchee-Gumee."
   Superior, they said, never gives up her dead
   When the gales of November come early!

Bottle of Wine

[*Words and music by* TOM PAXTON]

Tom Paxton is one of the few songwriting contemporaries of Bob Dylan who remains active today. Performing on the Greenwich Village folk scene of the 1960s, Paxton was performing this song when two members of Jimmy Gilmer and the Fireballs heard him sing it. They recorded their version in 1968, and the record was produced by Norman Petty, Buddy Holly's old record producer. The song was a hit and remains a staple in Paxton's repertoire.

Moderately, with a lilt

To verses
Final ending
G7 C G7 C
Let me go back and start o - ver. o - ver.
Verses:
C G F C
1. Ram - bl - in' 'round this dirt - y old town,
2. Pain in my head, bugs in my bed,
3. Preach - er will preach, teach - er will teach,
G7 C
Sing - in' for nick - els and dimes;
Pants are so old that they shine;
Min - er will dig in the mine;
G F C
Times get - tin' rough, I don't have e - nough to
Out on the street, tell the peo - ple I meet,
I ride the rods trust - ing in God,
G7 C
Play 3 times
get a lit - tle bot - tle of wine.
Buy me a bot - tle of wine.
Hug - gin' my bot - tle of wine.

Blowin' in the Wind

[*Words and music by* BOB DYLAN]

Blowin' in the Wind" is considered to be one of the primary anthems of the U.S. Civil Rights Movement and Bob Dylan's best-known song. Peter, Paul and Mary made the original hit recording in 1963, and hundreds of other artists have recorded the song since then. Sam Cooke was inspired to write his own powerful song, "A Change Is Gonna Come," after hearing Dylan's song. In 1999, the song was inducted into the Grammy Hall of Fame.

Brightly

1. How man - y roads must a man walk
2. How man - y times must a man look
3. How man - y years can a moun - tain ex -

down be - fore you call him a
up be - fore he can see the
ist be - fore it's washed to the

man? Yes, 'n' how man - y
sky? Yes, 'n' how man - y
sea? Yes, 'n' how man - y

seas must a white dove sail have be -
ears must one man have be -
years can some peo - ple ex - ist be -

fore she sleeps in the sand?
fore he can hear peo - ple cry?
fore they're al - lowed to be free?

Yes, 'n' how man - y times must the
Yes, 'n' how man - y deaths will it
Yes, 'n' how man - y times can a

can - non balls fly be - fore they're
take till he knows that too man - y
man turn his head pre - tend - ing he

for - ev - er banned?
peo - ple have died?
just does - n't see?

The

International Folk Songs

Ach! Du Lieber Augustin

[TRADITIONAL]

This song is an odd contrast between the rather jolly melody and the despairing lyrics that describe the plague and the hero's loss of his money and his girlfriend.

Black Is the Color

[TRADITIONAL]

Originally a Scottish folk song, this tune has been collected all over the Appalachian Mountains. John Jacob Niles rewrote the lyrics, and Nina Simone recorded a version with another set of lyrics.

Very slowly

Cockles and Mussels

MOLLY MALONE

[TRADITIONAL]

This song is also known as "Molly Malone." Molly Malone, the heroine mentioned in the lyrics, is commemorated by a statue at the bottom of Grafton Street in Dublin. Although there were many women named Molly Malone, it is not clear that any of them was the person portrayed in the song. The song was published during the 1880s and credited to James Yorkston of Edinburgh.

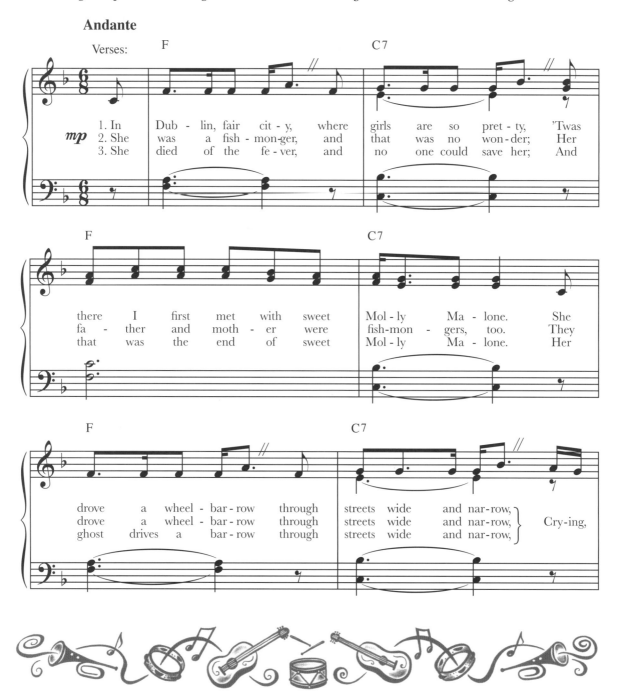

Andante

Verses:

1. In Dub - lin, fair cit - y, where girls are so pret - ty, 'Twas there I first met with sweet Mol - ly Ma - lone. She drove a wheel - bar - row through streets wide and nar - row, Cry-ing,

2. She was a fish - mon-ger, and that was no won-der; Her fa - ther first and moth - er were fish-mon - gers, too. They drove a wheel - bar - row through streets wide and nar-row, Cry-ing,

3. She died of the fe - ver, and no one could save her; And that was the end of sweet Mol - ly Ma - lone. Her ghost drives a bar - row through streets wide and nar-row, Cry-ing,

All through the Night

[*Words by* JOHN CEIRIOG HUGHES, *music* TRADITIONAL]

Written in 1784, this melody is representative of the distinguished Welsh choral music tradition.

Gently, like a lullaby

Alouette

[TRADITIONAL]

Although some scholars believe the original version of "Alouette" to be French, a printed version of it appeared in songbook published in Montreal in 1879. There are several Canadian versions, all of which commemorate the plucking of a lark's feathers. Each verse in turn describes the plucking of a new part of the bird, such as the head, neck, and feet.

Mary Anne

[TRADITIONAL, *new words, and music adapted by* JACQUELYN REINACH *and* DAN FOX]

Mary Anne" is a calypso song that supposedly celebrates the end of World War II. Various songwriters from Trinidad, including The Roaring Lion and The Mighty Sparrow, claim to have written it, and the melody has been traced to an old French song. The version printed here carries on the tradition of providing original words to this catchy melody; these lyrics are by Jacquelyn Reinach.

Moderate Calypso beat

All day, all night, Mar-y Anne,

Down by the sea-shore sift-in' sand.

All the lit-tle chil-dren love Mar-y Anne, 'Cause she can

Blow the Man Down

[TRADITIONAL]

The melody to this sea shanty has been traced to a German Christmas carol, and many sets of lyrics have turned up. The word "blow" means strike. One singer would line out the lyric, and the crew would respond with the refrain "blow the man down."

With a rollicking beat

1. Come, all you young fel - lows who fol - low the sea,
2. As I was a - walk - ing down Par - a - dise Street,
3. Says she then to me, "Sir, will you stand a treat?"

Way, hey, blow the man down; Now A "De -

pray pay at - ten - tion and lis - ten to me,
pret - ty young dam - sel I chanced for to meet,
light - ed," says I "for a charm - er so sweet."

Give me some time to blow the man down.

Auld Lang Syne

[*Words by* ROBERT BURNS, *music* TRADITIONAL]

This song is a fixture at midnight celebrations commemorating the new year. The Scottish poet Robert Burns wrote the lyrics in 1788, which he set to a traditional Scottish song. The lyrics were essentially traditional, yet they were partially based on a much earlier poem by Roybert Ayton.

Not too slow

Greensleeves

[TRADITIONAL]

Legend has it that King Henry VIII wrote "Greensleeves" for his future queen Anne Boleyn. Although this theory has never been proven, we know that the tune is found in various English manuscripts dating from the sixteenth and seventeenth centuries. The melody is used with a different set of lyrics in the Christmas song "What Child Is This?" Among the many recordings of "Greensleeves" are those made by John Coltrane, Lorena McKennett, Jethro Tull, and Sarah McLachlan.

3. I bought thee petticoats of the best,
   The cloth so fine as it might be;
   I gave thee jewels for the chest,
   And all this cost I spent on thee.
   (repeat chorus)

4. Well, I will pray to God on high
   That thou my constancy may'st see;
   And that yet once before I die,
   Thou will vouchsafe to love me.
   (repeat chorus)

Danny Boy

[*Words by* FRED WEATHERLY, *music* TRADITIONAL]

Oddly enough, Irish music scholar Michael Robinson has traced this song to a Scottish tune from the 1740s. "Danny Boy" is sometimes called "Londonderry Air." That name refers to the seventeenth-century colonization of Northern Ireland by English settlers. Robinson found that hundreds of lyrics have been composed to this tune. Among the dozens of recordings are those by Sinead O'Connor, Bing Crosby, Johnny Cash, Willie Nelson, Judy Garland, and Elvis Presley.

Slowly and freely

1. Oh, Dan-ny Boy, the pipes, the pipes are call-ing, From glen to glen and down the moun-tain-side. The sum-mer's gone and all the ros-es fall-ing, It's you, it's

2. But when ye come and all the flow'rs are dy-ing, If I am dead, as dead I well may be, Ye'll come and find the place where I am ly-ing, And kneel and

La Cucharacha

[TRADITIONAL]

The English translation of the title of this song is "the cockroach." The original version of the song was published during the Mexican Revolution, although the melody derives from an older traditional Spanish song. Some music historians claim that the song was a humorous depiction of the frequent breakdowns of an unreliable car driven by the famed general Pancho Villa.

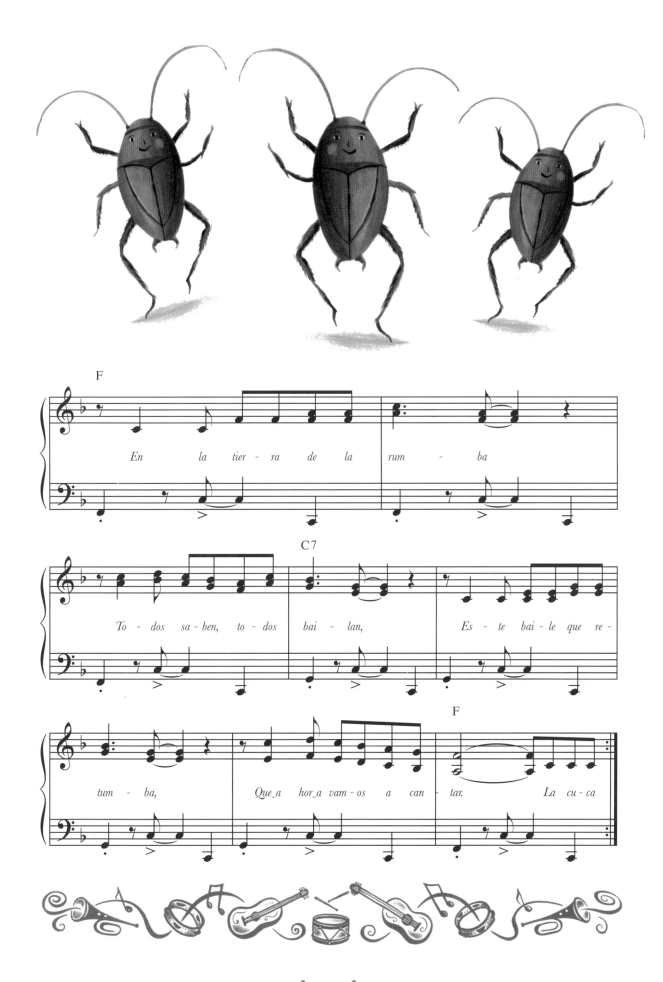

Hava Nagilah

[TRADITIONAL]

Composed as a celebration of the British victory in Palestine in 1918, the music of "Hava Nagila" is an ancient folk tune, and the text is variously attributed to Abraham Zive Idelsohn and M. Nathanson. The joyous melody is a celebration of Jewish life, and the Hebrew words translate to "Let us rejoice and be happy, Awake, brothers and sisters, With a happy heart!" "Hava Nagila" has been recorded by such stylistically varied artists as Harry Belafonte, heavy-metal band Anthrax, and surfing guitar hero Dick Dale. The melody has also been used as an instrumental by several others.

Loch Lomond

[TRADITIONAL]

Loch is a Gaelic word for a body of water that is either a lake or a sea inlet. Loch Lomond is the largest of the Scottish lochs, and its southern shore is about fourteen miles from the city of Glasgow. The song has been interpreted in a number of ways, but the most common explanation is that it concerns the capture of Prince Charlie's men after the failed uprising of 1745. The lyrics originated with a poem by Andrew Lang, published in 1876. The loch is referenced in the popular Lerner and Loew musical *Brigadoon*.

Chorus:

F   B♭   C7

Oh, ye'll take the high road and I'll take the low road, And

F   Dm   B♭   F   B♭   F

I'll be in Scot-land a-fore ye; But me and my true love will

B♭   Gm   C7   F   B♭   F   C7   F

nev-er meet a-gain On the bon-nie, bon-nie banks of Loch Lo-mond.

I Know Where I'm Going

[TRADITIONAL]

This song migrated from its Scottish birthplace to the United States. It has become a favorite with American folksingers, and Harry Belafonte, Judy Collins, and Burl Ives have recorded it.

Slowly and rather freely

3. Feather beds are soft,
   And painted rooms are bonny;
   But I'd leave leave all
   For my handsome, winsome Johnny.

4. Some say he's black,
   But I say he's bonny;
   Fairest of them all
   Is my handsome, winsome Johnny.

5. Repeat first verse

Drunken Sailor

[TRADITIONAL]

This song was first published around 1825. Its rousing chorus is ideal for singing while raising or lowering the sails or when weighing anchor. Verses were improvised as the work continued.

Boisterously

CONTINUE SIMILARLY:

2. Put him in the longboat till he's sober,
   Put him in the longboat till he's sober,
   Put him in the longboat till he's sober
   Earlye in the morning.
   (repeat chorus)

3. Dip 'im in the drink until he's sober,
   Dip 'im in the drink until he's sober,
   Dip 'im in the drink until he's sober,
   Earlye in the morning.
   (repeat chorus)

Scarborough Fair

[TRADITIONAL]

Simon and Garfunkel popularized this old English ballad under the name "Parsley, Sage, Rosemary and Thyme," in a 1966 recording. Paul Simon had learned the song from Martin Carthy, a highly respected British folksinger. Scarborough is a town in northwest England that was once a thriving seaport. The fair refers to a fifteen-day trading event that drew people from miles away.

Not too slowly

1. Are you go - ing to
2. Tell her to make me a
3. Tell her to wash it in

Scar - bor-ough Fair?
cam - bric shirt;
yon - der well;

Pars - ley, sage, rose -

mar - y and thyme.

Re - mem - ber
With - out an - y
Where nev - er spring

Chords above staff (top system): F   E m   D m   C

Lyrics (top system):
me   to   one who lives   there,   For
seam   or   nee - dle - work, fell,
wa - ter nor   rain ev - er

Chords (second system): D m   C   D m   C   D m   C

Lyrics (second system): once   she   was   a   true love of

Chords (third system): D m   D m add E

Lyrics (third system): mine.

After last
time only

pp

4. Tell her to dry it on yonder thorn,
   Parsley, sage, rosemary and thyme;
   Which never bore blossom since Adam was born,
   For she once she was a true love of mine.

5. Now he has asked me questions three,
   Parsley, sage, rosemary and thyme;
   I hope he will answer as many for me,
   For once he was a true love of mine.

6. Tell him to find me an acre of land,
   Parsley, sage, rosemary and thyme;
   Betwixt the salt water and the sea sand,
   For once he was a true love of mine.

7. Tell him to plough it with a ram's horn,
   Parsley, sage, rosemary and thyme;
   And sow it all over with one peppercorn,
   For once he was a true love of mine.

8. Tell him to reap it with a sickle of leather,
   Parsley, sage, rosemary and thyme;
   And bind it up with a peacock's feather,
   For once he was a true love of mine.

9. When he has done and finished his work,
   Parsley, sage, rosemary and thyme;
   O tell him to come and he'll have his shirt,
   For once he was a true love of mine.

The John B. Sails

[TRADITIONAL, *new lyrics by* DICK WEISSMAN]

The *John B.* was a ship that sank in the Bahamas, about 1900. The song was originally a traditional West Indian song, and was printed in 1927 in Carl Sandburg's *The American Songbag.*

Moderate Caribbean beat

Those Were the Days

[Words and music by GENE RASKIN]

Gene Raskin and his wife had a duo called Gene and Francesca, and they performed this song around New York City during the 1950s. The pop-folk group the Limeliters picked up the song in the early 1960s and, in 1968, Paul McCartney produced a major hit record of it with a then-unknown artist named Mary Hopkin. There were numerous cover versions, including a French version called "Le Temps Des Fleurs," which was a huge hit in Japan, Canada, and Greece.

Freely

1. Once up-on a time there was a tav-ern, We
2. Then the bus-y years went rush-ing by us;

Where we used to raise a glass or two. Re-
lost our star-ry no-tions on the way.

Last time, much slower

For we were young and sure to have our way.

La la la la la la la la la

la la la, Those were the days, Oh,

yes, those were the days.

3. Just tonight I stood before the tavern,
   Nothing seemed the way it used to be;
   In the glass I saw a strange reflection,
   Was that lonely fellow (woman) really me?
   (go to verse 4)

4. Through the door there came familiar laughter,
   I saw your face and heard you call my name.
   Oh, my friend, we're older but no wiser,
   For in our hearts the dreams are still the same.
   (repeat chorus)

Michael, Row the Boat Ashore

[TRADITIONAL]

This song dates back to Civil War days. It appears in *Slave Songs of the United States,* by Allen, Ware, and Garrison, which was published in 1867. It appears to have originated as a rowing song in the Georgia Sea Islands. The name "Michael," refers to the Archangel Michael.

Kum Ba Ya

[TRADITIONAL]

Reverend Martin Frey claimed to have composed this song in the 1930s, but a song called "Come By Yuh," sung in the Gullah language by the descendants of slaves, was collected earlier.

Moderately slow, but with a strong, steady beat

1. Kum ba ya, my Lord, kum ba ya; Kum ba ya, my Lord, kum ba ya; Kum ba ya, my Lord, kum ba ya, Oh, Lord, kum ba ya.
2. Some-one's call - ing, Lord, kum ba ya; Some-one's call - ing, Lord, kum ba ya; Some-one's call - ing, Lord, kum ba ya, Oh, Lord, kum ba ya.
3. Some-one's pray - ing, Lord, kum ba ya; Some-one's pray - ing, Lord, kum ba ya; Some-one's pray - ing, Lord, kum ba ya, Oh, Lord, kum ba ya.

CONTINUE SIMILARLY:

4. Someone's singing . . .
5. Someone's crying . . .
6. Help me, Jesus . . .
7. Kum ba ya, my Lord . . .

Barbara Allen

[TRADITIONAL]

This beloved ballad was found in the British Isles and transported to the United States. "Barbara Allen" first appeared in Francis James Child's ballad collection, categorized as "Child Ballad #84."

Slowly and very freely

1. In Scar - let Town, where I was born, There was a
2. All in the mer - ry month of May, When green buds
3. He sent his ser - vant to the town, He sent him

fair maid dwell - in'; Made ev - 'ry youth cry
they were swell - in' Sweet Wil - liam on his
to her dwell - in'; Say - in', "Mas - ter's sick, he is

well - a - day! Her name was Bar - b'ry Al - len.
death - bed lay For love of Bar - b'ry Al - len.
ver - y sick For love of Bar - b'ry Al - len."

4. Then slowly, slowly she got up,
   And slowly she came nigh him;
   And all she said when she got there,
   "Young man, I think you're dyin'."

5. When he was dead and in his grave,
   Her heart was filled with sorrow;
   "Oh, mother dear, go make my bed,
   For I shall die tomorrow."

6. And as she on her deathbed lay,
   Begged to be buried by him;
   And she repented of the day
   That she did e'er deny him.

7. "Farewell, farewell, ye maidens all,
   And shun the fault I fell in;
   So now take warning by the fall
   Of cruel Barbara Allen."

Guitar Instructional Tips

HOW TO USE THIS BOOK

The purpose of this section is to give the reader some suggestions about what sort of right-hand picking techniques work with the songs in this book.

Basic Guitar

The simplest and most basic way to play any of these songs is to strum across the strings with either your right thumb or, if you are using a pick, to pick down across the strings with a plectrum. If the song is in 4/4 time, you can either do this four times for each bar of music or you can use the strum in eighth note patterns and pick up and back with either your thumb or the pick, four times in each direction for every bar of music. If the song is in 3/4 time, play either three or six times, depending upon whether you are playing quarter or eighth note patterns.

Single Note and Chord Playing

In this right-hand pattern, the thumb plays a bass string, and the index finger plays down (away from your body) across the strings. If you are using a plectrum, play a single note and then strum down across the strings. In 4/4 time the pattern looks like this:

1. Thumb plays 6th or 5th string
2. Index finger brushes down across strings
3. Thumb plays 4th string
4. Index finger brushes down across strings
5. Thumb plays 6th or 5th string
6. Index finger brushes down across strings
7. Thumb plays 4th string
8. Index finger brushes down across strings

Remember, you can substitute the pick for the fingers, if you prefer to play that way. In 3/4 time the same pattern is used, but instead of eight steps, you will have six steps. In either case, all notes and strums are even eighth notes.

Expanding the Thumb-Index Pattern

Although the thumb-index pattern produces a richer sound than simply brushing with the thumb, it too is a fairly limited technique. To expand it, try the following strum, in 2/4 time:

1. Thumb plays 5th string
2. Index finger brushes down across strings
3. Index finger brushes back across strings
4. Thumb plays 4th string
5. Index finger brushes down across strings
6. Index finger brushes back across strings

The rhythm is now eighth note, followed by two sixteenth notes, eighth note followed by two sixteenth notes, or

    Bum ba ba Bum ba ba

If you use this strum in 4/4 time, there are twelve steps instead of six. If you use it in 3/4 time, there are nine steps. If you are playing with a flat pick on the third and sixth steps of the strum, you are playing toward you.

Arpeggios

An arpeggio is a series of individual notes, rather than strums. When you play the arpeggio, use the thumb and three fingers of the right hand. All the notes are even eighth notes. In 4/4 time the sequence goes like this:

1. Thumb picks down on 6th or 5th string
2. Index finger picks up on 3rd string
   (up means toward your body)
3. Middle finger picks up on 2nd string
4. Ring finger picks up on 1st string
5. Thumb picks down on 4th string
6. Index finger picks up on 3rd string
7. Middle finger picks up on 2nd string
8. Ring finger picks up on 1st string

If the arpeggio is in 3/4 time, the pattern changes to

1. Thumb plays 6th or 5th string
2. Index finger picks up on 3rd string
3. Middle finger picks up on 2nd string
4. Ring finger picks up on 1st string
5. Middle finger picks back (toward you) on 2nd string
6. Index finger picks back on 3rd string

Note:

Arpeggios can be played with a flat pick, but this is less effective than playing them with your bare fingers. Try to get as clear a sound as you can. It helps to keep your right hand arched and to play directly over the sound hole of the guitar. Notice that if you play near the bridge you get a brighter but harsher sound.

It is possible to create many more strums from the arpeggio pattern. For example, instead of playing thumb then index finger, you can play thumb followed by ring finger. You can also play occasional double notes, using, for example, the thumb and one of your other fingers playing together. You can either approach this mathematically, by simply writing out the strums, or spontaneously through experimentation.

Travis Picking

Travis picking is a right-hand technique named after the country guitar picker Merle Travis. The simplest form of Travis picking alternates the thumb with the index or middle finger. In 2/4 time play each note evenly (four equal eighth notes):

1. Thumb picks down on 6th or 5th string
2. Middle finger picks up on 1st string
3. Thumb picks down on 4th string
4. Index finger picks up on 1st string

To play this pattern in 4/4 time, simply repeat the four steps.

Although we have given the pattern in even eighth notes, it is also possible to make the thumb notes just slightly longer than the notes played with the index or middle finger. Country great Chet Atkins was fond of modifying the pattern by muting the thumb note.

As with arpeggio playing, it is possible to come up with many variations on the Travis patterns by using the thumb playing at the same time as one of the fingers or by making use of the ring finger. Many of the players who use Travis picking anchor their ring finger on the guitar or on the pick guard. This provides support but also prevents you from using the right-hand ring finger.

More Right-Hand Techniques

Advanced players will want to explore the many right-hand techniques used in contemporary guitar playing. Blues, flamenco, classical jazz, and rock guitar utilize their own particular methods to get the sounds appropriate for playing these varied musical styles. There are many fine guitar methods available; the reader might want to explore the New Age Guitar Series published by G. Schirmer, coauthored by the authors of this book. If you are interested in exploring improvisation, the authors have a current book out called *Non-Jazz Improvisation for Guitar*, published by Mel Bay.

Other Helpful Hints

There are far too many guitar instructional tips to list here. Many of the more current instructional books contain CDs or DVDs, which can be quite helpful in terms of playing along with the instructor or observing such matters as correct hand positions, use of a slide in slide guitar playing, etc. Playing with other musicians is almost always helpful. Most major cities have music stores that specialize in acoustic music, and these stores are a valuable resource for everything from guitar parts to taking lessons or meeting other guitarists.

Index

Credits